SECRETS OF COMPANION PLANTING

SECRETS

OF

COMPANION

PLANTING

by Louise Riotte

ILLUSTRATIONS BY THE AUTHOR

Garden Way Publishing *Charlotte, Vermont 05445*

Published in the United States by Garden Way Publishing, Charlotte, Vermont 05445.

Library of Congress Catalog Card Number: 75-3491
International Standard Book Number: 0-88266-064-0 paperback
International Standard Book Number: 0-88266-065-9-6 casebound

INTRODUCTION

The magic and mystery of companion planting has intrigued and fascinated men for centuries, yet it is a part of the gardening world that has never been fully explored. Even today we are just on the threshold, and in the years to come I hope men of science and gardeners and farmers everywhere will work together in making more discoveries that will prove of great value in augmenting the world's food supply. Already insect- and disease-resistant fruits, grains and vegetables are appearing, while experiments are being made on weed-resistant varieties.

Plants that assist each other to grow well, plants that repel insects, even plants which repel other plants—are all of great practical use. They always have been, but we are just beginning to find out why. Delving deeply into this fascinating facet of gardening can provide for us both pleasure and very useful information. I hope that what I have written here will give you many of the tools to work with.

It is important to remember that not all "protective" botanicals act quickly. For example marigolds, to be effective in nematode control, should be grown over at least one full season, and more is better, for their effect is cumulative. Nasturtiums grown in a fruit orchard should be plowed under later so that the trees can take up the protective exudates in the decomposing plants. On the other hand certain companion plants will diminish each other's natural repelling ability as they grow together. Both root secretions and odor are important in repelling or attracting.

7

A major enemy of the carrot is the carrot fly, whereas the leek suffers from the onion fly and leek moth. Yet when they live together in companionship the strong and strangely different smell of the partner plant repels the insects so much that they do not even attempt to lay their eggs on the neighbor plant. They take off speedily to get away from the smell. This is why mixed plantings give better insect control than a monoculture where many plants of the same type are planted together in row after row.

It's the same with kohlrabi and radishes in their community life with lettuce. Both are often afflicted by earth flies, but when the flies get the odor of lettuce they take flight. Even when plants are affected by diseases one usually can alleviate the situation by a mixed plant culture. All through this book you will find "what to grow with" and "what *not* to grow with." Both are equally important to gardening success.

Worth studying too, are the accumulator plants—those that have the ability to collect trace minerals from the soil. They actually can store in their tissues up to several hundred times the amount contained in an equal amount of soil. These plants, many of which are considered weeds, are useful in the compost pile, others as green manures, still others as mulch. But these plants must be allowed to decompose and be returned to the soil before food plants can make use of them.

Leaving the flowers and vegetables, we will come to an entirely different type of community life, that of fruit and nut trees and the bush and bramble small fruits. Have you ever experienced the disappointment of having a beautiful fruit tree blossom, then be visited by the bees, and yet have it fail to bear? There is a reason, of course, and it lies in pollinization.

Pollen is the dust from blossoms that is needed to make the plant fruitful. If the tree is self-unfruitful and there is no pollenizer of the correct type growing near, it is doubtful that the tree will ever bear well. In the chapter on pollinization I'll attempt to unravel some of this mystery which seems particularly to plague new gardeners and orchardists.

And if a fruit tree dies should you replace it with another of the same kind? Never. Remember the story about the farmer who took his cattle to the same pasture year after year. In time, due to the manure dropped, there were some particularly green spots, yet the animals refused to eat this grass. One day he pastured his horse and some sheep in the meadow and found they ate the grass with gusto. For them it was good pasturage.

A young apple tree planted where an old apple tree was removed withered and died. Yet a young cherry put in exactly the same spot grew like a weed. Why? Because the root and leaf secretions left in the soil by the old apple tree worked poisonously on the young apple. But for the cherry tree it was welcome nutrition.

And, lastly, I will go into poisonous plants. This chapter is not meant to frighten but to warn, for most of the nursery catalogs do not tell us which plants are poisonous or in what degree. Even some of the gardening encyclopedias do not.

Cases of death resulting from poisonous plants are rare, but they do happen. In the ABC's of companion gardening I have cited from time to time such poisonous plants that are useful in the garden for various reasons. It is only fair to tell you that some of those most commonly used may be harmful to children, to livestock or even to you.

Many of our loveliest and most useful plants are poisonous— the Christmas poinsettia, oleanders, daffodils, scillas, lily-of-the-valley, hyacinth and larkspur. Other equally poisonous plants are of value for medicines or as insect repellents. To know is to be forewarned, and we still may use them. And poisonous plants unlike poisonous insects or animals are never aggressive. You are in control of them at all times.

All of the suggestions given in this book for companion planting are only a beginning. Your own experiments will lead you into many exciting pathways and discoveries.

THE ABC'S OF
COMPANION PLANTING

A

Absinthium (*Artemisia absinthium*). Also called wormwood, this plant is grown as a border to keep animals from the garden. Ornamental species such as *A. pontica,* have leaves of great delicacy and are good to plant in flower beds and around choice evergreens.

Alder (*Alnus tenufolia*). Closely related to the hornbeams and birches is this small, water-loving tree that grows very rapidly and serves definite, special uses. The genus *alnus* includes twenty species, nine of which grow in North America and six of which reach the height of trees. Alders may be planted in hedges along the borders of streams where their closely-interlacing roots hold the banks from crumbling and keep the current clear in midstream. Alders are also of assistance in draining wet soils.

In America the black alder is often found in horticultural varieties. The daintiest are the cut-leaved forms, of which *imperialis,* with leaves fingered like a white oak, is a good example.

Alfalfa (*Medicago sativa*). This is one of the most powerful nitrogen-fixers of all legumes. A good stand can take 250 pounds of nitrogen per acre from the air each year. Alfalfa needs a deep soil

11

without a hardpan or an underlying rock layer, because it sends its roots down very deep. Researchers have traced them for well over one hundred feet, and 20 to 30 feet is average.

Alfalfa's deep-rooting ability is the source of its great nutritional power, feeding as it does from mineral-rich subsoil which has not been worn out and depleted. Alfalfa is strong in iron and is also a good source of phosphorus, potassium, magnesium and trace minerals.

You can easily sprout alfalfa seeds in the kitchen, and you may even want to grow some in your garden for highly nutritious alfal-fa greens, or use its leaves for tea. Used as a meal it is a great com-post stimulant and activator, particularly good for composting household garbage.

Alfalfa will make good growth where dandelions grow. Dande-lions themselves are deep divers, their presence indicating the sub-soil is easy to penetrate. Alfalfa grown in pastures will give pro-tective shelter for shallower rooting grasses, keeping other plants alive longer during spells of dry weather. As a trap crop alfalfa will draw lygus bugs away from cotton. Two percent alfalfa provides sufficient control, but it should be planted about a month before the cotton.

Algae.   Here is a food source not yet fully explored, and which may prove of great value as populations increase, for the total amount of photosynthesis carried on by marine algae may be ten times greater than the total of such activity in all land plants. If this is true then we may well look to the plants of the sea as a rich, abundant and relatively untapped source of foodstuffs.

In some parts of the world, for example, Japan and China, algae for many years have been important items in the human diet. Farmers in many coastal regions cultivate brown algae on bamboo stems pushed into the ocean bottom in shallow waters. Dried prep-arations of this brown algae, available in many food stores in the United States, are very rich in minerals and also have moderate quantities of carbohydrates and vitamins. Brown algae because of their rich mineral content, also are often used as soil fertilizers (spread on fields and plowed under), or they may be dried and burned and their ash used as fertilizer. Some species are a commercial source of iodine for medicinal use.

Allelochemics. This, the study of chemical interactions between species, is a new and rapidly expanding field of ecology. There *is* a transmission between organisms of extremely powerful natural chemical substances. The organism receiving the message is compelled to take a certain action, and an amount of the messenger substance, as small as one molecule, can produce an effect a great distance from its source. Negative or inhibiting influences of plants on one another, is called *allelopathy*. The technical names of substances causing interactions between species are:

PHEROMONES. These are the chemical messengers used for communication between individual organisms of the same species. A stinging bee will die because it cannot extricate its stinging organ, but when this happens it releases a pheromone which tells other bees to come and sting also. Sex pheromones are released by many insects to help them find mates.

ALLOMONES. These are similar substances which can be understood by individuals of different species. Generally speaking allomones will cause a plant, insect or animal to perform a function beneficial to itself. These functions can include repellent or escape substances, venoms, prey and pollination attractants.

KAIROMONES. These too form part of the language between species, but are detrimental in their purpose. Black walnuts, sycamores, chaparral and certain maples are thought to release a substance, washed from their leaves, which "tells" other plants not to grow around their roots. It has been observed that if the upper portions of such trees are devasted by a fire, released herb seeds will grow until such time as the trees or shrubs grow again and release the inhibiting substance.

Allium (*Allium*). Flowering onions belong to the lily family, *Liliaceae*. Actually allium is a Latin word for garlic. Vegetable alliums are chives, garlic, leek, onion and shallot but there are ornamental alliums as well which are excellent to plant with roses, protecting them from aphids and many other pests. They thrive on the same care and culture as onions and are very easy to grow. Alliums also repel moles.

Flowering onions like plenty of compost but will do well even on dry soil. Some of the larger varieties such as Jewel of Tibet grow to a height of five feet and have a blossom head up to eight inches in diameter. Flowering onions come in many colors besides blue and purple—in greenish-white, yellow, rose and dark red. The larger varieties should be staked in windy climates. Alliums are winter hardy and may be left in place year after year. (See SUPPLIER LIST for allium sources.)

Aloe Vera (*Aloaceae*).   Nature's own medicine plant, known and used for centuries, is a vegetable belonging to the lily and onion family. The name "aloe vera" means "true aloe" and it is so named because, among 200 species of aloe, it has the best medicinal properties.

The aloe family belongs to a larger class of plants known as the *xeroids,* so called because they possess the ability to close their stomata completely to avoid the loss of water. The plants are easy to grow outside in warm climates which are frost free, and equally easy to grow indoors in pots. Possibly because of the bitter taste of the gel, they appear to be completely disease and insect free. Almost all xeroids are laxative in nature and have a bitter flavor.

Young aloe vera plants come up at or near the base of the parent plant. Unlike cactus, its thorns are soft and may be touched without harm. Powdered aloes dusted on plants repel rabbits.

Aloin is the thick, mucilaginous yellow juice which occurs at the base of the aloe leaves, and is also present in the rind. The gel may be removed from the leaf as one would filet a fish. It is a very slippery and clear, viscous juice useful for sunburns, for healing cutaneous ulcers of radioactive origin as well as burns and scalds of various types. The gel is taken by thousands of people for stomach ulcers. Many fishermen carry aloe vera aboard their boats to stop the pain of a sting from a Portugese Man-of-War. It also will stop the sting often experienced when gathering okra.

The gel may be used instead of tree wound dressing if it becomes necessary to cut a tree limb. The surface will heal over quickly and insects are repelled by the bitter taste. The juice may be mixed with water to make a spray for plants. Powdered aloes dusted on young plants will repel rabbits, but this must be repeated after rain. Aloe vera plants, thrown in the drinking water for chickens, is said to cure them of certain diseases. (See SUPPLIERS INDEX for sources.)

Amaranth (*Amaranthus retroflexus*). This plant, sometimes called *rough pigweed* and commonly found in disturbed ground everywhere, is one of the best weeds for pumping nutrients from the subsoil. It is especially good to grow with potatoes but must be

Pigweed is one of the best for pumping nutrients from the subsoil. It's of particular benefit to potatoes, onions and corn but must be kept thinned.

kept thinned or the potatoes will be choked out. Amaranth is beneficial to grow with onions and corn, too.

Euell Gibbons in his *Stalking the Healthful Herbs* says that green amaranth has a higher iron content than any other green vegetable except parsley.

A type of amaranth grown widely in rural Mexico is known as "The sacred food of the Aztecs." The small seeds, easily threshed from the large heads, can be baked with bread. Sometimes they are even popped, mixed with honey and eaten as a confection. In India certain species are eaten as a salad or cooked like spinach, and the seed is ground into flour.

Amaranth (which is distantly related to beets) has a higher protein content, is higher in vitamin C and has approximately the same amount of vitamin A as the cultivated beet.

Anise (*Pimpinella anisum*). The spicy seeds of this annual herb, related to caraway and dill, are used to flavor licorice as well as pastry, cookies and certain kinds of cheese. The oil extracted from the seeds is used to make absinthe, and it is also used in medicine. The flower, powdered and infused with vermouth, is used for flavoring muscatel wine. Anise is antiseptic with oils of peppermint or wintergreen and is useful as an ointment (when mixed with lard) for lice and itching from insect bites.

When sown with coriander, anise seed will germinate better, grow more vigorously and form better heads.

Ant (*Formicidae*). Ant pollination has been observed by a Pennsylvania biologist James C. Hickman, in a small annual plant, *Polygonum cascadense*. Previously it had been believed that ants play little if any role in pollination. It presently is believed that ants pollinate only plants that grow close to the ground, and then in hot, dry areas where ants are most abundant.

Ants have always had a reputation for spreading aphids, mealybug, white flies, scale insects and leafhoppers. This is true, for ants feed on the honeydew secreted by these insects, and in turn they protect them from their natural enemies, from parasites and predators that would normally keep them down.

However, some species of ants are known controllers of insect pests. For centuries Chinese citrus growers have placed ants in orchards to prey on caterpillars and other pests, even providing them with bamboo runways from tree to tree.

If ants are a problem in the kitchen they may be repelled with pennyroyal and spearmint scattered on shelves. Mints or tansy planted near doorways and around the house also act as repellents.

Aphid (*Aphididae*). Aphids come in a wide spectrum of colors and may be green, black, pink, yellow or red. These soft-bodied insects attack and injure almost all plants, stinging them and deforming their leaves.

Nasturtiums will keep broccoli aphid free. Clumps of chives planted between chrysanthemums, sunflowers or tomatoes will discourage them. Ants bring the aphids, but tansy will discourage the ants.

Ladybugs are the enemies of aphids. I have frequently observed them working on okra blossoms when there is an occasional infestation in my garden.

Although aphids injure plants when they are present in great numbers, still it would be a mistake to eradicate them completely. Some must remain for the aphid-eating insects to feed on.

Spent plants of Chinese celery cabbage attract aphids and are useful for this purpose as a trap crop. If nasturtiums are planted in a circle around fruit trees, aphids will avoid them. A scientist at

Small braconid wasp stings a grain-destroying aphid and inserts an egg in its body. The wasp larva destroys the aphid.

Artichokes - water, juice of one lemon + cardamon Seeds — french dressing

The aphis lion or lace wing fly is pale green. Its larva, at left, devours many aphids.

the Connecticut Experiment Station found that the yellow color of the nasturtium blossoms causes flying aphids to avoid plants growing *above* them.

Asparagus (*Asparagus officinalis*).   Parsley planted with asparagus gives added vigor to both. Asparagus also does well with basil, which itself is a good companion for tomatoes. Tomatoes will protect asparagus against asparagus beetles because they contain a substance called *solanine*. But if asparagus beetles are present in great numbers, they will attract and be controlled by their natural predators, making spraying unnecessary. A chemical derived from asparagus juice also has been found effective on tomato plants as a killer of nematodes, including root-knot sting, stubby root and meadow nematodes.

In my garden I grow asparagus in a long row at one side. After the spears are harvested in early spring I plant tomatoes on either side, and find that both plants prosper from the association. Cultivating the tomatoes also keeps down the weeds from the asparagus. The asparagus fronds should never be cut, if at all, until very late in the fall as the roots need this top growth to enable them to make spears the following spring.

Aster (*Asteroides*).   Many asters are soil indicators. Some like low, moist soil. So if the bushy type (*Boltonia asteroides*), or the purple-

stemmed (*A. puniceus*) show up in your pastures or fields they indicate a need for drainage. The sea aster (*A. tripolium*), grows on
seasides and near salt mines and is a salt and soda collector. The
poisonous woody aster (*Xylorhiza parryi*), of the West indicates an
alkaline soil.

Auxins. These are hormones that stimulate plant growth. Buds,
embryos, young leaves and the tips of stems produce auxins that
make the plants grow rapidly. These hormones also are responsible for plants growing toward light. Light falling on one side of
the stem will cause the auxins to move away from the light and
accumulate in the shaded portion of the stem. Then the increased
number of auxins in the unlighted portion will cause greater
growth of the cells on the shaded side. Because the cells on the
shaded side grow longer than those on the sunny side, the stem
gradually bends toward the light.

Auxins are horticulturally valuable by stimulating root formation on cuttings, to prevent potatoes from sprouting or to prevent
leaf drop on some plants and others to defoliate before harvest.
Gibberellic acid is one of several auxins which stimulate the
growth of plants. Scientists believe that the gibberellins are natural plant products. These substances make plants grow larger, induce blossoming, and speed up seed germination. They also seem
to promote the growth of trees and agricultural crops. Many plants
are stimulated to grow much taller.

Since the effect of companion plants upon one another depends
largely upon root exudates, nitrogen-fixing ability, odor, etc., it
appears that growth regulators such as auxins have only a mild
effect, one way or another.

Azelea (*Ericaceae*).   Azeleas, holly, pieris and rhododendrons are
good companions for a landscape planting because all like humusy, acid soil. Do not plant azeleas or rhododendron near black walnut trees. The substance, called juglone, washed from the leaves
of black walnuts is detrimental to them.

B

Bacillus Thuringiensis.   This is a selective bacterial disease, effective against many insects including the fruit tree leaf roller. During spore production, bacillus thuringiensis produces crystals that act as a stomach poison on the insects eating the treated plants. This substance is not toxic to plants, man or other animals and can be applied even up to the day of harvest.

It is also highly effective against caterpillars and the larvae of moths, as well as tent caterpillars—the disease attacking the pest in the caterpillar stage after they have come out of the tent. The disease is widely used to protect commercial crops of celery, lettuce, cabbage, broccoli, cauliflower, mustard, kale, collards, and turnip greens. It is also effective against the tobacco budworm and the bollworm. (For sources see SUPPLIERS INDEX.)

Basil (*Ocimum basilicum*).   As noted under Asparagus, basil helps tomatoes to overcome both insects and disease, also improving growth and flavor. Since this is a small plant, one to two feet tall, grow it parallel to the tomatoes rather than among them. Basil also repels flies and mosquitoes.

Sweet basil has inch-long, dark green leaves and a clove-pepperish odor and taste. Pinch out the plant tops and they will grow into little bushes, the dwarf varieties especially becoming beautifully compact. As a kitchen herb, basil is used in vinegar, soup, stew, salad, with cottage cheese, egg or tomato dishes, chopped meat, sausage, and may be sprinkled over vegetables. Dark Opal makes a very handsome house plant.

It has been known since ancient times that basil and rue dislike each other intensely. Perhaps this is because basil is sweet and rue is very bitter.

Bay (*Lauris nobilis*).   Bay (or laurel) leaves put in stored grains such as wheat, rice, rye, beans, oats and corn will eliminate weevils.

The bay belongs to the same family as the cinnamon, camphor, avocado and sassafras trees. I have tried sassafras leaves in grains and flours and find them also effective against insects and weevils.

Bean (*Phaseolus* and *Vicia*).   Many different kinds of beans have been developed, each with its own lore of "good" and "bad" companions. Generally speaking, however, all will thrive when interplanted with carrots and cauliflower, the carrots especially helping the beans to grow. Beans grow well with beets, too, and are of aid to cucumbers and cabbages.

A moderate quantity of beans planted with leek and celeriac will help all, but planted too thickly they have an inhibiting effect, causing all three to make poor growth. Marigolds in bean rows help repel the Mexican bean beetle.

Summer savory with green beans improves their growth and flavor as well as deterring bean beetles. It is also good to cook with beans.

Beans are inhibited by any member of the onion family—garlic, shallots or chives—and they also dislike being planted near gladiolus.

Broad beans are excellent companions with corn, climbing diligently up the corn stalks to reach the light. They not only anchor the corn more firmly, acting as a protection against the wind, but a heavy vine growth may also act as a deterrent to raccoons. Beans also add nitrogen to the soil which is needed by the corn.

Bean and Potato.   Bush beans planted with potatoes protect them against the Colorado potato beetle. In return the potatoes protect the bush beans from the Mexican bean beetle. It is considered best to plant the beans and potatoes in alternate rows.

Bean, Bush (*Phaseolus vulgaris*).   Included with bush beans are those known as butter, green, snap, string or wax beans. All will do well if planted with a moderate amount of celery, about one celery plant to every six or seven of beans.

Bush beans do well also when planted with cucumbers. They are

in rows next to summer savory

garlic every 4 or 5 ft. nasturtium + summer savory

mutually beneficial. Bush beans planted in strawberry rows are mutually helpful, both advancing more rapidly than if planted alone.

Bush beans will aid corn if planted in alternate rows. They grow well with summer savory but never should be planted near fennel. They also dislike onions, as do all beans.

Bean, Lima (*Phaseolus limensis*).   Nearby locust trees have a good effect on the growth of lima beans. Other plants give them little or no assistance in repelling insects. Never cultivate lima beans when they are wet, because if anthracnose is present, this will cause it to spread. If the ground has sufficient lime and phosphorous there will probably be little trouble from anthracnose and mildew.

Bean, Pole.   Like others of the family, pole beans do well with corn and summer savory but they also have some pronounced dislikes such as kohlrabi and sunflower. Beets do not grow well with them but radishes and pole beans seem to derive mutual benefit.

Beebalm (*Monarda*).   Improves both the growth and flavor of tomatoes.

Beech (*Fagus*).   Beech trees and ferns often grow together, and scilla bulbs do well under the trees. Beech trees in their infancy do well under the shade of other trees so each fruiting tree is the mother of many young ones.

Beet (*Beta vulgaris*).   Beets grow well near bush beans, onions or kohlrabi but are "turned off" by pole beans. Field mustard and

Beets and kohlrabi make good companions. Both take the same kind of culture too, and they take soil nourishment at different levels.

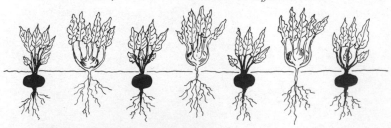

charlock inhibit their growth. Lettuce and most members of the cabbage family are "friendly" to them.

Birch (*Betula*).   It is believed that birch roots excrete substances which make the trees useful to plant around manure and compost piles by encouraging fermentation. Dr. Ehrenfried Pfeiffer, one of the early advocates of the Bio-Dynamic Method of farming and gardening, observed that composts fermented in the vicinity of the gray birch derived benefit from it and suffered no losses of nutrients even if the roots actually penetrated the heap. It is considered best, though, to maintain a distance of at least six feet from the tree when building a compost pile.

Birds.   Birds around the garden are generally recognized as one of the best controls against insect pests, particularly the purple martins which must catch flying insects almost constantly in order to live. Well-made martin houses set up away from large trees will

The purple martins rid orchards and garden areas of incalcuable numbers of injurious insects, devouring them in the winged stage.

attract Martin colonies. Feeders and bird waterers will also encourage other birds to visit and nest near your garden.

Birds are particularly attracted to hackberry, chokecherry, elderberry, Tartarian honeysuckle, mulberry, dogwood, Japanese barberry, red and black raspberries, viburnum, Hansen bush cherry, Russian olive, hawthorne and sunflowers. Evergreen trees and thorn bushes are attractive for nest-building. In this respect certain forms of cactus are attractive in the Southwest.

Birds, however, can be too much of a good thing at times and may become very destructive to the food plants we grow for ourselves. From the Chinese we have this suggestion: When fruits start to ripen, hang sliced onions in the trees—the birds dislike the scent and will avoid the fruit. Hanging empty milk cartons in fruit trees from a string so they twirl in the breeze will deter many birds. Change their position occasionally, and perhaps also use bright, fluttering ribbons or strips of cloth.

If crows are a problem for a corn or watermelon patch put up several stakes and string white twine around the patch, criss-crossing it through the center. To the birds this will look like a trap and they will avoid the patch.

Black Alder (*Ilex verticillata*).   Black alders along with willows help to drain wet soil. The root nodules also add nitrogen to the soil, the black alder being the only nonleguminous plant which is able to perform this function.

Blackberry (*Rubus allegheniensis*).   Mulberries, chokecherries and elderberries may be used to attract birds away from valued blackberry crops. Blackberries themselves are strong vital plants that help in preparing the soil to support the growth of trees. (See chapter on POLLINATION.)

Black Fly (*Aphididae*).   This insect is particularly detrimental to broad beans, and it is advisable to use a fermented extract of nettle to keep it under control, while its natural enemy, the lady beetle, will help. Intercropping with garlic, or placing an occasional plant of nasturtium, spearmint or southernwood in the rows of beans also is a good plan.

Black Nightshade (*Solanaceae*).   Where black nightshade grows profusely the soil is tired of growing root crops. This plant also draws the Colorado potato beetle away from potatoes since they prefer the weed, though it is poisonous. The beetles eat it and die.

The nightshade family includes apple of sodom, belladonna, bittersweet, capiscum, eggplant, jimson weed (*datura*), petunia, potato, solanum, snakeberry, tobacco and tomato.

Borage (*Boraginaceae*).   This is an excellent provider of organic potassium, calcium and other natural minerals. Grow this herb in orchards and as a border for strawberry beds. Honeybees like to feast on the blossoms.

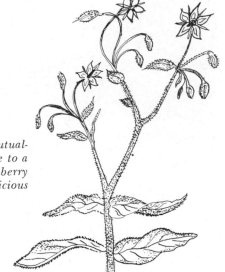

Borage and strawberries are mutually helpful, but limit the borage to a few plants at the side of the berry bed. Borage juice make a delicious and healthful drink.

Border Plants. Castor beans planted around the perimeter of the garden will repel moles, while borders of daffodil, narcissi, scilla and grape hyacinths around flower beds will discourage mice. If used in small amounts dead nettle (henbit), sainfoin, esparsette, hyssop, lemon balm and valerian are helpful to all vegetables. Yarrow is a good plant in paths, as well as borders, as it will grow well even if walked upon. Planted as a border to the herb garden it enhances the growth of essential oils in the herbs.

Borers. Nasturtiums planted around fruit trees repel borers, while garlic and other alliums such as onions or chives also are good.

Botanical Sprays. *Pyrethrum* flowers (*Chrysanthemum cinerariafolium* or *C. Roseum*), may be dried on sheets of newspapers in a well ventilated place. Pulverize it to a powder and mix with water for spraying.

ROTENONE comes from the derris root. Soak the roots overnight in a small amount of water, crush them the next day and return to water and boil. The resulting extract is the insecticide. Roots and rhizomes of hellebore, which control a number of leaf-eating insects, may be used the same way.

NICOTINE. Tobacco and its main alkaloid, nicotine, has been used as an insecticide since the late Seventeenth century, but it dissipates rapidly when sprayed or dusted. Nicotine sulfate, highly diluted in water with a soap solution added to make it adhere and spread better, is more lasting. Both substances are highly toxic to mammals as well as insects and should be handled very carefully.

QUASSIA. The quassia tree, a native to South America, is intensely bitter and this quality makes it effective as an insecticide.

RUE, the bitterest of herbs, is an excellent insect repellent for the same reason, deterring the Japanese beetle when planted near roses and raspberries.

RYANIA, a Latin American shrub and native to Trinidad, does not always kill insects outright but rather puts them into a state of paralysis, causing them to stop feeding.

SABADILLA. All extracts of this plant are harmless except the seeds, which when heated or treated with an alkali become toxic to many insects. Oddly enough this quality increases with age during storage. The extract is effective against a large group of insects such as grasshoppers, corn borer, codling moth, webworm, aphid, cabbage looper and squash bug. Be cautious in handling the dust and do not breathe it in.

OIL SPRAYS. Properly used and at the right time, dormant oil sprays are effective, particularly in orchards, against many chewing and sucking insects. The oils make a tight film over insect eggs causing suffocation. Apply only in early spring over leafless trees. (See also BACILLUS THURINGIENSIS, CHIVE, ELDERBERRY, GARLIC, GRASSHOPPER, HORSERADISH, HORSETAIL, LAVENDER, MILKY SPORE DISEASE, MUGWORT, NASTURTIUM, PARSNIP, PEPPER, RHUBARB, SAGE, STINGING NETTLE, TOBACCO, TOMATO, WHITE HELLEBORE.)

Broccoli (*Brassica oleraceae*). Like all members of the cabbage family broccoli does well with such aromatic plants as dill, celery, camomile, sage, peppermint, rosemary, and with other vegetables such as potatoes, beets and onions. Do not plant it with tomatoes, pole beans or strawberries. Use pyrethrum on broccoli against aphids but before the flower buds open.

Broom Bush (*Sarothamnus vulgaris*). This useful weed grows on the poorest, stoniest soils and those that are sandy and slightly to medium acid. Being rich in calcium carbonate, the plant improves the soil through decomposition of its leaves and stems. In a thin stand it will provide shelter for young tree seedlings, but it will choke them out if too many of the weeds are present.

Buckwheat (*Fagopyrum esculentum*). Buckwheat is valuable as a soil builder and it will grow on very poor soils while collecting lots of calcium. Used in this manner it not only will take the light away from low-growing weeds, choking them out, but if plowed under as green manure it will sweeten the soil and make it more suitable for growing other crops. Buckwheat does not like winter wheat.

Bulbs. Autumn flowering bulbs such as crocus and colchicum (which are poisonous if eaten), are very attractive but often are simply allowed to come up without an accompanying ground cover. They are much prettier if low growing companion plants such as white alyssum, phlox subulata, *P. divaricata,* armeria, saponaria, common thyme or vinca minor, are used as a framing ground cover.

Burdock (*Arctium*).   Do not allow wild burdocks to grow since they are robbers of the soil. Particularly do not allow them to go to seed, for the burrs will adhere to the hair of sheep, horses, dogs, even clothing, and be spread far and wide.

Burdock roots have medicinal value and are said to alleviate gout and skin diseases. An edible burdock (*Takinogawa*) has been developed in Japan, where the cooked roots are greatly relished for their refreshing, pungent flavor. The Orientals also value this burdock for its reputed blood-purifying qualities and the relief it is said to give to sufferers of arthritis. (It is available from NICHOLS GARDEN NURSERY.)

Butternut (*Juglans cinerea*).   See WALNUT.

C

Cabbage (*Brassicaceae*).   The cabbage family includes not only cabbage but cauliflower, kale, kohlrabi, broccoli, collards and Brussels sprouts—even rutabaga and turnip. While each plant of this group has been developed in a special way, they are all pretty much subject to the same likes and dislikes, insects and diseases. Hyssop, thyme, wormwood and southernwood are helpful in repelling the white cabbage butterfly.

All members of the family are greatly helped by aromatic plants, or those which have many blossoms, such as celery, dill, camomile, sage, peppermint, rosemary, onions and potatoes.

If rabbits dig your cabbage patch, plant any member of the onion family among them. Or you can dust with ashes, powdered aloes or cayenne pepper. Rabbits also shun dried blood or blood meal.

Cabbages dislike strawberries, tomatoes and pole beans. All members of the family are heavy feeders and should have plenty of compost or well-decomposed cow manure worked into the ground previous to planting. Mulching will help if soil has a ten-

Butterflies themselves do no harm and can help pollinate plants. It is their hatched eggs which as caterpillars do such damage to the orchard and field crops. The white cabbage butterfly is perhaps the most destructive. Herbs will repel them: hyssop, peppermint, rosemary, sage, thyme and southernwood.

Dill improves flavor

wood ashes when moths appear. tar paper at base for maggots

dency to dry out in hot weather, and water should be given if necessary.

Cabbage and cauliflower are subject to clubroot, and if this occurs try new soil in a different part of the garden. Dig to a depth of 12 inches and incorporate plenty of well-rotted manure into the soil. Rotate cabbage crops every two years.

If cabbage or broccoli plants do not head up well it is a sign that lime, phosphorus or potash is needed. Boron deficiency may cause the heart of cabbage to die out.

Calamus (*Araceae*).   It is said that mosquitoes are never found in swamps or other standing water in which calamus, sometimes called sweetflag or sweet root, is growing.

Calcium.   Peas, beans, cabbages and turnips revel in soil containing lime, but a few plants—notably those belonging to the heath family, such as erica, azalea and rhododendrons—actually dislike it. Potatoes and a few cereals are not at their best if lime is applied to the ground immediately before they are planted or sown.

Land in need of lime does not respond to cultivation and manuring as it should, and often coarse weeds such as sheep sorrel flourish. Sometimes a green scum grows over the surface. A soil test that reveals excessive acidity indicates the need for liming.

Buckwheat accumulates calcium, and when composted or plowed under as green manure enriches the soil. Lupine (*Lupinus*) has roots which penetrate to surprising depths even on steep, gravelly banks or exposed sunny hills. They add calcium to the soil, too, and are of value to grow on poor, sandy soils worthless for other purposes.

Scotch broom, a member of the legume family, also accumulates calcium but may become a weed unless kept in check. Melon leaves are rich in calcium and should be added to the compost heap when the plants are spent.

Calendula (*Calendula officinalis*).   See MARIGOLD.

Camomile helps both the flavor and growth of cabbages and onions. It has a pleasant smell and is used in hair rinses.

Camomile (*Chamomile*). The real plant, the German or wild camomile (*Matricaria chamomilla*) recognizable by the hollow bottom of the blossom and its highly aromatic odor, often is confused with Roman camomile (*Anthemis nobilis*). This is an excellent companion to cabbages and onions, improving growth and flavor of both. But it should be grown sparingly, only one plant every 150 feet.

Wheat grown with camomile in the proportion of 100 to 1 will grow heavier and with fuller ears, but too much will harm field crops too.

Camomile contains the substance *chamazulene,* which has anti-allergic and anti-inflammatory properties when used in the form of tea.

The tea will calm a cranky baby and it is also used for diarrhea or scours in calves. A tea of one-third each camomile, lemon balm and chervil applied as a warm compress will cure hoof rot in animals.

Camomile flowers may be used in the dog's bed against fleas. When using herbs in pet pillows simply add herbs to pillow stuffing, occasionally adding more to freshen up.

The blossoms soaked in cold water for a day or two can be used as a spray for treating many plant diseases and to control damping off in greenhouses and cold frames.

A camomile rinse is excellent for blond hair. Use 3 or 4 table-spoons of dried flowers to a pint of water. Boil 20 to 30 minutes, straining when cool. Shampoo hair before using, since it must be free of oil. Pour rinse over hair several times and do not rinse with clear water after using. It will leave the hair smelling like sweet clover.

Camomile contains a hormone which stimulates the growth of yeast. Grown with peppermint in very small quantities it increases their essential oil.

Caraway (*Carum carvi*).   Though it is difficult to sprout caraway seed, sow it with a companion crop of peas. After harvesting the peas, harrow the area and the caraway will come up. It's good to plant on wet, heavy land, the long roots making an excellent sub-stitute for subsoiling. Do not grow fennel near it.

Europeans like and use caraway seed more often than we do. It is put in rye bread for its aromatic flavor and to make it more digestible. It is also used in cakes, cheeses and apple and cabbage recipes.

Carrot (*Daucus carota*).   For sweet-tasting carrots your soil must have sufficient lime, humus and potash. Too much nitrogen as well as a long period of hot weather will cause poor flavor.

Carrots are good to grow with tomatoes—also with leaf lettuce, chives, onions, leeks, radishes, rosemary and sage. Tomatoes' other friends in-clude chives, onions, parsley, asparagus, marigold and nasturtiums. To-matoes do not like potato, kohlrabi, fennel or cabbage.

Onions, leeks and herbs such as rosemary, wormwood and sage act as a repellent to the carrot fly (*Psila rosae*) whose maggot or larva often attacks the rootlets of young plants. Black salsify (*Scorzonera hispanica*), sometimes called oyster plant, also is effective in repelling the carrot fly. Use as a mixed crop. Carrots grow well with leaf lettuce and tomatoes but have a pronounced dislike for dill. Carrot roots themselves contain an exudate beneficial to the growth of peas.

Apples and carrots should be stored a distance from each other to prevent the carrots from taking on a bitter flavor.

Castor Bean (*Ricinus communis*). Experiments have shown that castor beans planted around a garden will repel moles, and they also are good to repel mosquitoes.

This is an agricultural crop in some areas where it is grown for the oil in the seed, yet all parts of the plant are poisonous to livestock and humans, particularly the seed. Two or three seeds eaten by a child can be fatal and as few as six can cause the death of an adult. The beans also carry an allergen that causes severe reactions in some people when handling castor pomace. This danger

Castor beans are poisonous, especially the seeds, but around the garden are said to repel moles and also mosquitoes.

can be eliminated if the seed heads are clipped off or destroyed before they mature.

To be most effective as a mole repellent plant castor beans every five or six feet around the perimeter of the garden. Use them also as another companion crop. Plant several pole lima beans close to their base and let them climb the tall growing plants. The largest variety of castor bean, *Zansibarensis*, grows 8 feet tall, has large leaves and beautiful variegated seeds of various colors. *Sanguineus* grows 7 feet tall and *Bronze King* five feet. (See SUPPLIERS INDEX.)

Catch Cropping.   This simply means growing a quick-to-mature crop of some vegetable in ground you've reserved for a planting of a later or slower growing crop such as tomatoes or a member of the cabbage family such a broccoli or cauliflower. While you are waiting put in radishes, lettuce or spinach as catch crops.

Catnip (*Nepeta cataria*).   Catnip contains an insect repellent oil, *nepetalactone,* and fresh catnip steeped in water and sprinkled on plants will send flea beetles scurrying.

The catnip compound is chemically allied to those found in certain insects. Two of these occur in ants and another in the walkingstick insect, which ejects a spray against such predators as ants, beetles, spiders, birds and even humans. Freshly-picked catnip placed on infested shelves will drive away black ants. But my cats love catnip, and I like to eat it in salads.

Cauliflower (*Brassicaceae*).   The white cabbage butterfly (*Pieris rapae*) is repelled if celery plants are grown near the cauliflower, but cauliflower does not like tomatoes or strawberries. Extract from cauliflower seeds inactivate the bacteria causing black rot.

Celeriac (*Apium graveolens rapaceum*).   A sowing of winter vetch before planting celeriac is helpful, for the plant needs a rich, loose soil with plenty of potassium. The leek, also a potassium lover, is a good companion in alternating rows as are scarlet runner beans.

Celeriac does not need as much attention as celery since blanching is not necessary, but as the root starts to enlarge the crown may be helped to better development and higher quality by removing the fine roots and the soil attached to them. Many lateral roots close to the top of the crown tend to make the fleshy part irregular and coarse.

Celery (*Apium graveolens*).   Celery grows well with leeks, tomatoes, cauliflower and cabbage, while bush beans and celery seem to give mutual assistance. One gardener believes that celery is particularly benefited if grown in a circle so that the lacy, loosely interwoven roots may make a more desirable home for earthworms and soil microbes. Celery and leeks both grew well when trenched. Both celery and celeriac are reported to have a hormone which has an effect similar to insulin, making them an excellent seasoning for diabetics or for anyone on a salt-reduced diet.

Celery dinant or French celery dinant is a unique type that sends out a multitude of narrow thin stalks. I have found it easy to grow here in southern Oklahoma, that it has a much fuller flavor than common celery and less should be used in cooking.

This celery is completely insect-free and grows well with all garden vegetables. Plants will freeze in winter but the root does not and will put out new leaves from the center with the advent of warm spring weather. In a cold climate the leaves may be dried for winter use.

Charlock (*Brassica arvensis*).   Charlock or wild mustard is frequently found in grain fields. The seeds and those of wild radish can lie inert in the ground for from 50 to 60 years, showing up again when the field is planted to grain, particularly oats.

Chayote (*Sechium edule*).   This is a perennial tropical vine, an annual in colder climates, which bears a delicious, light green, pear-shaped fruit in the fall. Two vines must be grown or it will not bear well. Chayotes in a cream sauce are a dish "fit for the gods." I grow them on my garden fence along with cucumbers, where both do exceptionally well. They apparently have no insect enemies and seem to be protective to the cucumbers.

Cherry (*Prunus avium*).   Wheat is suppressed by the roots of cherry trees, and potatoes grown in the vicinity are less resistant to blight.

Chervil (*Anthriscus cerefolium*).   This is one of the few herbs that will grow better in partial shade. Rosetta E. Clarkson in her *Herbs, Their Culture and Uses,* says that it is best shaded by taller plants growing near it. She also says that it does not take kindly to transplanting. Chervil is a good companion to radishes, improving their growth and flavor.

Chestnut (*Castanea*).   It is well known that the chestnut blight has just about wiped out the native American species. An experiment reported by Alfred Szezo of Oakdale, New York states that American chestnut trees planted very close to Chinese and Japanese trees have shown significant increases in blight resistance. American chestnuts also have shown greater blight resistance when grown in hardwood forests closely associated with oaks. This is an interesting area for further experiment.

Chilo Iridescent.   This virus has been evaluated at the Arkansas Experiment Station and found to be stable and effective against both the tobacco budworm and the boll weevil.

Chinese Celery Cabbage (*Brassica chinensis*).   This easy-to-grow vegetable, deserving to be better known in America, is one of the oldest vegetable crops in China. I grow both types: the tall, slender

Chinese celery cabbage is good in the fall garden, does well interplanted with Brussels sprouts.

heads and the huge, deeply savoyed hybrid type (*Burpee*) which makes a round head. I find celery cabbage grows well, making enormous heads, if planted in my fall garden about two feet apart. I alternate the plants in the row with Brussels sprouts or cauliflower.

Celery cabbage has few insect enemics but should not be grown near corn as the corn worms will infest it.

Chive (*Allium schoenoprasum*).   Chives are a good companion to carrots, improving both growth and flavor. Planted in apple orchards they are of benefit in preventing apple scab, or made into chive tea may be used as a spray for apple scab or against powdery mildew on gooseberries and cucumbers.

Chlorophyll.   A team of scientists directed by R. S. Alberte of Duke University has studied the reasons why some plants like light, shade, a warm climate or a cool one. This was done by evaluating the exact amounts of two plant pigments found under various temperatures. The pigments, chlorophyll *a* and chlorophyll *b*, are directly responsible for the photon-tapping ability of plant chloroplasts. They found that temperature seems to affect the ratio of one pigment to the other. Such ratios, in turn, affect the quantity and composition of the photosynthetic units and, by so doing, affect the plant's ability to capture sunlight and change it into usable plant sugars.

This is of great importance because in time it may be possible to tailor plants to specific and diverse environments by improving the photosynthetic efficiencies of our most necessary food crops. Strains also may be developed which will grow well in either warmer or cooler climates.

Chromatography.   This useful laboratory method for separating mixtures of substances usually is done with a column formed by a glass tube packed with absorbent materials such as alumina, silica gel and cellulose.

The substance to be analyzed first must be made into a solution which is poured onto the top of the absorbent material forming the column. Components of the sample solution are absorbed near the top of the column.

The chemist then adds a solvent to wash the absorbed components of the sample through the column. He must select a solvent that affects only the substance being analyzed and not the material forming the column. The components move through the column at varying rates of speed finally to separate as distinct zones or bands. After this it is possible to identify and measure the amount of each component. If the components are colored they will appear as bands of colors.

Chromatography has been used to explain the mystery of why cucumbers like beans and beans dislike fennel. Plant extracts were mixed and chromatograms made on them individually as well as in solutions together. Beans, cucumbers and fennel alone gave a chromatogram of good detail, shape and color. A test of the "good" companions (beans-cucumbers) resulting in a composite chromatogram showed an enhancement of the good features of both. The peculiar design of the beans was still present, but both chromatograms were intensified, made stronger and more viable. However, when beans and fennel were tested together the resulting "picture" was dull, muddy and indistinct.

The late Dr. Ehrenfried E. Pfeiffer who originated the Sensitive Crystallization Method, as suggested by Dr. Rudolf Steiner, made many tests on a number of different substances including chemical fertilizers and compost. The chemical yielded chromatograms that were dull and lifeless but the ones made from compost were brilliant with color. Could this have been because of the *living* microorganisms contained in the compost? This supposition seems logical.

It is possible to make a specific chromatographic test to find out why, or if at all, a plant is helping or hindering its neighbors.

Cinquefoil (*Potentilla monspeliensis*). The cinquefoils are considered a bad symptom when found on pasture land, for they indicate a very acid soil, and gradually they will choke out other grasses and clovers. They are very persistent and will last when other

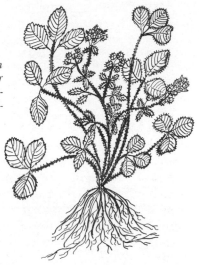

It's bad news if you see cinquefoil on your land, but clover and other grasses will choke it out, while butternut trees and black walnuts inhibit its growth.

grasses are burned out by drought. It has been observed that the butternut or gray walnut tree (*Juglans cinerea*) and the black walnut have an inhibitory effect on the growth of the creeping cinquefoil.

Citrus (*Citrus*). Lime, lemon, orange and grapefruit trees grow better in the area of guava, live oak or rubber trees, which apparently exert a protective influence.

Climate. Since climates vary greatly throughout the world, where you live should always be taken into account when you plan your garden. Maximum summer and minimum winter temperatures should be considered, as well as annual rainfall. For best success try plants recommended for your area, making these your garden basics. This determined, you can then have fun experimenting each year with a few borderline plants, those that do best in either a warmer or colder climate. Often by providing shelter or otherwise creating a "mini" climate you may grow these successfully. Some natural feature of your land, such as a pond, may enable you to grow something that your neighbor, a few miles away cannot. Mulching to keep the ground cool for certain plants may be helpful. Improving soil with humus often makes it possible to grow vegetables or plants that formerly were unsuccessful. Winter protection will help in the North, shade or a windbreak in the South.

Clover (*Leguminosae*).   Planting clover between rows of grapes will add nitrogen to the soil. This also works well in orchards or with companion grasses. Clover dislikes henbane and also members of the buttercup family, which secrete a substance in their roots that inhibits the growth of nitrogen bacteria and poisons the soil for clover. This poisoning is so effective that clover will disappear in a field if buttercups are increasing. Clover has a stimulating effect on the growth of deadly nightshade (*Solanum nigrum*).

Cockroach (*Blatella*).   Extracts of chinaberry have been found useful against cockroaches and termites. The little known cockroach plant (*Haplophyton cimicidum*) from Mexico also is valuable in controlling this pest.

Collard (*Brassica oleracea,* var. *acephala*).   Cornell University's College of Agriculture has shown that collards benefit from interplanting with tomatoes since the flea beetle, the prime pest of collards, was significantly decreased.

Collards, widely grown in the southern states as a source of greens, are more nutritious than heading cabbage, and their taste is improved by freezing.

Columbine (*Aquilegia vulgaris*).   These beautiful plants are very attractive in some areas to red spiders, so keep them in the flower bed and out of the vegetable garden. Columbines grown in humus-rich soil are less susceptible to damage by leaf miners. They will grow well in combination with rhubarb if both are given plenty of well-rotted cow manure. Columbines are strong growers themselves but do not assist other plants and often are detrimental. They are heavy feeders, so if you want to grow them as ornamentals give them plenty of compost and feed other plants grown in their vicinity equally well.

The Indians considered flowers of wild columbine (*A. canadensis*) as effective a tranquilizer as librium is today.

Comfrey (*Symphytum officinale*).   Comfrey, also called knitbone or healing herb, is high in calcium, potassium and phosphorus, rich in vitamins A and C. It was an ancient belief that comfrey preparations taken internally or as a poultice bound to injured parts hastened the healing of broken bones.

It is possible that the nutrients present in comfrey actually do assist in the healing process since we now know that the herb also contains a drug called allantoin, which promotes the strengthening of the lining of hollow internal organs.

The very first leaves of comfrey, gathered in the early spring, are quite delicious to eat, but let the later ones go. The leaves of Russian comfrey are ideal for the compost heap, having a carbon-nitrogen ratio similar to that of barnyard manure.

Compost.   Compost is largely composed of decayed organic matter which has heated sufficiently to kill weed seeds and then has thoroughly decomposed. Plant preparations may be used to influence or speed up the fermentation process, and these—even when added in small amounts—can influence the entire operation. Once conditions are right earthworms enter the compost pile and assist the other microorganisms in the breaking-down process.

Certain plants such as stinging nettle may be used to speed up or assist fermentation in the compost heap or manure pile. It is an excellent soil builder and like comfrey also has a carbon-nitrogen ratio similar to barnyard manure. Nettles also contain iron.

Other herbs particularly well endowed with minerals and which can be of value incorporated into compost, are dandelion which absorbs between two and three times as much iron from the soil as other weeds; salad burnet with its rich magnesium content; sheep sorrel which takes up phosphorus; chicory, goosegrass and bulbous buttercup which accumulate potassium. Horsetail shares honors with ribwort and bush vetch for a capacity to store cobalt. Thistles contain copper as a trace element.

Compost is the best fertilizer for herbs as well as garden vegetables and is particularly rich if weeds are put in the pile instead of being destroyed. Use all herb refuse obtained in the garden, too, and naturally all the kitchen waste, particularly in a household where cooking with herbs is a frequent feature.

Any organic material can be added, but refuse of a woody nature will decompose more rapidly if it is crushed or chopped first and used as a base mixed with materials such as grass clippings. Leaves picked up in the fall make good compost, but since they are apt to pack they should be mixed with other material. Bulky materials form a solid mass of rotting vegetation, lack oxygen and quickly become sour and greasy.

When making a pile the site first should be well dug to allow for a quick entry of earthworms. Incorporate sods into the heap. Build your pile up to a height of about six feet with straight sides and a slightly concave top. The contents must be kept moist and allowed to heat so that weed seeds are killed. The quicker the heating the earlier the heap should be turned and restacked.

Turpentine substances, washing from the leaves of conifers, will retard fermentation. Birch trees in the vicinity assist fermentation, even if their roots penetrate the heap. It is best, however, to have them at least six feet away.

Conifer (*Coniferae*).   Turpentine substances washing from the leaves of conifers such as pine trees will inhibit the fermentation process of compost piles. Interplanting onions with conifers will

Squirrel damage in pines and others trees can be limited by planting onions nearby.

help prevent damage by squirrels, which eat the buds of Scotch, white and red pines. Plant winter-hardy Egyptian onions.

Pine needles make an attractive mulch and will increase the stem strength, flavor and productiveness of strawberries. In general conifers have an adverse effect on the growth of wheat, since rain washing over them contains substances which inhibit the germination of seeds.

Coreopsis (*Calliopsis*). Coreopsis in the flower bed is useful as an insect control for nearby plants. It also is an attractive annual (of the Compositae family) whose yellow, red or maroon flowers grow on tall, slender stems. It looks like daisies and may have one or two layers of petals.

Coriander (*Coriandrum sativum*). Coriander has a reputation for repelling aphids while being immune to them itself. It helps anise to germinate but hinders the seed formation of fennel. In blossom the herb is very attractive to bees.

Many people think the foliage and fresh seed of coriander has a disagreeable smell, but as the seeds ripen they gain a delicious fragrance which intensifies as they dry. The savory seeds, sometimes sugar-coated as a confection, are baked in breads or used to flavor meats.

Coriander has four times more carotene than parsley, three times as much calcium, more protein and minerals, more riboflavin and more vitamin B_1 and niacin. Oil of coriander is used medicinally to correct nausea.

Corn (*Zea mays*). Sweet corn does well with potatoes, peas, beans, cucumbers, pumpkin and squash. Research has shown that to remove corn suckers is a waste of time as well as being detrimental to the development of the ears. Peas and beans help corn by restoring to the soil the nitrogen used up by the corn. Is there anyone who hasn't heard the story of Indians putting a fish in every corn hill?

Melons, squash, pumpkins and cucumbers like the shade provided by corn. In turn they benefit the corn, protecting it from

white geranium - no jap beetles. Trichogamma wasp
Honeycross - Burpee - born borers + lady bugs

the depredations of raccoons, which do not like to travel through the thick vines. Similarly pole beans may be planted with corn to climb on the stalks. But don't plant tomatoes near corn because the tomato and corn warworm are identical.

An experiment with *odorless* marigold showed that when it was planted next to corn the Japanese beetles did not chew off the corn silks.

An experiment reported in the British *New Scientist* in 1970 states that, "Reduced incidence of fall armyworm on maise (corn) and a correspondingly increased yield were obtained by growing the crop with sunflower in alternating strips . . . there were also large reductions in the numbers of Carpophilus beetles in the sunflower strips, compared with unbroken areas of the crop. Some infestations were cut by more than half."

Cornflower (*Centaurea cyanus L.*).   Cornflowers, in the proportion of 1 to 100 seeds, are noted for their salubrious effect when grown with rye. They also are beneficial to other small grains if grown in about the same proportion.

The cornflowers or bachelor's buttons supply bees with nectar even in the dryest weather. They are beneficial to growing rye, too, but in limited numbers.

It was a custom among Russian peasants to decorate the first sheaf of the rye harvest with a cornflower wreath, after which it was placed in front of an icon. Cornflowers, whose other names are bachelor's button and bluebottle, also are noted for supplying bees with abundant nectar even in the driest weather.

Cows. Cows give more and better milk when fed on nettle hay, and marjoram fed to cows is thought to prevent abortion. A tea made of balm and marjoram is helpful after calving. Do not let sneezeweed (*Helenium autumnale*), sometimes called swamp sunflower, grow in pastures. Most cows respect the bitter leaves, but many a pail of milk has been spoiled by a mouthful of helenium among the herbage. If you are wondering why this plant is called sneezeweed, take a whiff of snuff made from the dried and powdered leaves.

Other plants that should never be allowed to grow in pastures are the field and the meadow garlic (*Allium vineale* resp. *canadense*). Just a few minutes after a cow has eaten some field garlic her entire body is penetrated, and after half an hour the milk is flavored with it and remains so for several hours. To avoid damage to the milk it may be necessary to keep the cows off the pasture or let them graze for only a short time after milking, then removing them to another pasture.

Larkspur is a plant that is poisonous to cattle.

Cotton (*Gossypium*). Alfalfa planted before cotton will put nitrogen in the soil, to the cotton's benefit, and alfalfa planted with it will discourage root rot. A virus, *Chilo iridescent,* has been found effective against the boll weevil.

Cotton growers try to keep the pink bollworm under control by isolating infected fields, sterilizing seeds and cotton, and by using machines that chop up leaves and other trash from the cotton. Shredding stalks in late summer and plowing them under helps control the worm and the boll weevil.

Farmers now protect their crops against the diseases of older cotton plants by growing varieties that are bred to resist such diseases as wilt and blight. For additional information see *Insect Resistance in Crop Plants* by Reginald H. Painter, professor of entomology at Kansas State University.

Crab Grass (*Digitaria sanguinalis*).   If crab grass shows up in the garden try to conquer it by frequent cultivation. In a lawn good fertilization will enable the more desirable grasses to grow vigorously.

Crowfoot (*Ranunculaceae*).   The common meadow buttercup is one of this family which secretes a substance in their roots that poisons the soil for clover by inhibiting the growth of nitrogen bacteria. So potent is this secretion that clover in time will disappear if buttercups begin to invade the field. Cattle will not eat the acrid, caustic plant, and children should be warned against biting the buttercup's stem and leaves, which are capable of raising blisters.

The garden monkshood (*Aconite*) is even more dangerous, being poisonous in all its parts, while other members of this family which are more or less poisonous are delphinium, columbine and peonies. They are beautiful, but grow them with care.

Cucumber (*Cucumis sativus*).   Cucumbers apparently are offensive to raccoons, so they are a good plant with corn. And corn seemingly protects the cucumbers against the virus that causes wilt. Thin strips of cucumber will repel ants.

Cucumbers also like beans, peas, radishes, and sunflowers, and, preferring some shade, they will grow well in young orchards. Sow two or three radish seeds in cucumber hills to protect against cucumber beetles. Do not pull the radishes, but let them grow as long as they will, even blossoming and going to seed. Cucumber beetles also may be trapped by filling shallow containers about three-fourths full of water into which some cooking oil has been poured.

If cucumbers are attacked by nematodes try a sugar spray. I boil a half cup of sugar in two cups of water, stirring until completely dissolved. Let cool and dilute with a gallon of water.

Strange as it seems, sugar kills nematodes by drying them out. This will also attract honeybees, insuring pollination and resulting in a bumper crop of cucumbers, so the spray is worth trying even if you don't suspect the presence of nematodes.

Beneficial fungi are another enemy of nematodes. If you suspect their presence, build up the humus content of your soil. A chive spray is helpful for downy mildew on cucumbers as is a spray made of horsetail (*Equisetum arvense L.*). (See HORSETAIL.)

Cucumbers dislike potatoes, while potatoes grown near cucumbers are more likely to be affected by phytophthora blight, so keep the two apart. Cucumbers also have a dislike for aromatic herbs.

Plant scientists William Duke of Cornell and Alan Putnam of Michigan State have discovered that certain cucumber varieties fight weeds by releasing a toxic substance. This natural process, allelopathy, is believed to be an inherited trait. Thus attempts are being made to incorporate weed-resistance into commercial crops much in the same way as insect and disease resistance is bred into plants. They are now working to isolate the plant genes that produce the weed-inhibiting substance.

Cutworm (*Noctuidae*).   A three inch cardboard collar around young plants extended one inch into the ground and two inches above will foil cutworms. Use cardboard cut from toilet paper or paper towel rolls or cut off the top and bottom from a quart size milk carton and cut the remainder into three collars.

A used matchstick, toothpick, small twig or nail set against the plant stem will keep the cutworm from wrapping itself around the plant and cutting it. Oak leaf mulch will repel cutworms, too.

Cypress Spurge (*Euphorbia cyparissias*).   This funny little plant escaped from Eastern gardens where it was grown as an ornamental. The milky juice once was thought to be effective against warts, and it is used in France as a laxative. Here the plant has become a weed. Do not let it grow near grapes, since it may cause the vines to become sterile, and cattle eating hay containing the spurge are made ill.

D

Damping-off Fungi.   This is a disease caused by fungi, apparently present in the soil, which kills many young plants. It is characterized by collapse of the stems, or the seedlings falling over. It may occur before the seeds germinate or after the seedlings emerge. To avoid this, potting soil in which seeds are planted should be treated to kill the fungi by steam heating the soil to 180 degrees F. for one-half hour or more. A simple method for the home gardener is dry heating the soil in an oven. Place the soil 4 to 5 inches deep in a pan and bury a small potato about 1 1/2 inches in diameter in it. Bake in 200-degree oven until the potato is done, and the soil is sterilized and ready to use.

Dandelion (*Taraxacum officinale*).   Dandelion is considered one of the "dynamic" weeds since it likes a good, deep soil as do clover and alfalfa. Soil around dandelions is liked by earthworms, for this

thick leaved
25 plants

Dandelions really don't compete with lawn grasses. They bring minerals up from the subsoil and their deep roots make channels for the earthworms, while being beneficial to growing alfalfa.

plant is a natural humus-producer. Dandelions on your lawn may frustrate, but actually they are not in competition with the grasses because of their three-foot deep roots. They bring up minerals, especially calcium, from beneath the hardpan which they penetrate, depositing them nearer the surface thus restoring what the soil has lost by washing. When dandelions die their root channels act like an elevator shaft for earthworms, permitting them to penetrate deeper into the soil than they might otherwise.

Dandelions exhale ethylene gas which limits both the height and growth of neighboring plants. It also causes nearby flowers and fruits to mature early.

Datura (*Datura stramonium*).   Other names for this weed are Jamestown weed, jimson weed, apple of Peru, thorn apple, stinkweed, devil's trumpet, angel's trumpet and dewtry. Although all parts of datura are poisonous it is a source of valuable medicine. The weed is especially helpful to pumpkins and it protects other plants from Japanese beetles. The smoke from dried datura leaves is calming to honeybees when opening a hive, but use it sparingly.

Daylily (*Hemerocallis*).   If you have a slope or terrace too steep to mow, try planting daylilies and iris together. Their roots will hold the soil and their blossoms, which arrive successively (the iris blooming first), will delight you all summer.

Daylilies are unaffected by the "juglone" washed from the black walnut's leaves. The flower buds are delicious dipped in batter and fried.

Not generally known is the fact that daylilies are a tasty food. Buds and blossoms can be sautéed in butter with a little salt and used alone or added to a zucchini and tomato dish. They may also be dipped in batter and fried. They may even be dried for later use in soups and stews.

Dead Nettle (*Lamium album*).   Although classed as a nettle this plant, sometimes called white archangel, has no relation to stinging nettle and does not sting. A similarity of the leaves may be the reason for its name. This plant has a long season of showy white bloom and is one of the few herbs that will also grow in damp places in filtered sunlight. As such, it is a valuable companion for the garden and also for grain crops.

Devil's Shoestring (*Tephrosia virginiana*).   There are nineteen species of this native North American weed that have valuable insecticidal properties. It is low in toxicity to animals, but is reputed to contain a fish poison. Wild turkeys are fond of eating the plant.

Diatomaceous Earth.   This effective remedy against many insects is made from the finely-ground skeletons of small, fossilized one-celled creatures called diatoms, which existed in the oceans and constructed tiny shells about themselves out of the silica they extracted from the waters. The microscopic shells, deposited on the floor of the ancient seas, collected into deposits sometimes thousands of feet deep.

This earth contains microscopic needles of silica which do their work by puncturing the bodies of insects, allowing vital moisture to escape from them. The insects die from dehydration. This earth is so finely milled that it poses no threat to either humans or animals, but these particles, when taken internally by insects, interfere with breathing, digestion and reproductive processes.

Diatomaceous earth will not harm earthworms, which are structurally different from the insects. The earthworm's outside mucus protection, coupled with its unique digestive system, enables it to move through soil treated with diatomaceous earth without harm. Many gardeners use diatomaceous earth as a dusting agent to give effective control against gypsy moth, codling moth, pink boll weevil, lygus bug, twig borer, thrip, mites, earwigs, cockroach, slugs, adult mosquitoes, snails, nematodes, all species of flies, corn worm, tomato hornworm, mildew and so on. For field crops and in orchards the diatomite particles are best applied with an electrostatic charger which gives the particles a negative charge, causing them to stick to plant surfaces. (For source see SUPPLIERS INDEX.)

Dill (*Anethum graveolens*). Dill is a good companion to cabbage, improving its growth and health. It does not do well by carrots and if allowed to mature will greatly reduce that crop. So pull it before it blooms.

Dill will do well if sowed in empty spaces where early beets have been harvested, and light sowings may be made with lettuce, onions or cucumbers. Honeybees like to visit dill blossoms. *Tomatoes / it repels green tomato worm*

Disease and Weather-resistant Vegetable Varieties:
ASPARAGUS: *Mary Washington,* rust resistant (Farmers)
BEAN: *Topcrop, Tendercrop, Harvester,* mosaic-resistant (Twilley Seed Co.). *Wade,* mosaic and powdery mildew-resistant (Farmers)
BEAN, DRY SHELL: *Michlite,* blight-resistant (Farmers)
CABBAGE: *Stonehead Hybrid,* yellows-resistant (Burpee). *Wisconsin Hollander No. 8; Copenhagen; New Wisconsin Ballhead, Wisconsin All Season,* yellows-resistant (Shumway)
CUCUMBER: *Marketmore,* scab and mosaic-resistant. *Polaris,* anthracnose, downy mildew and powdery mildew-resistant (Twilley). *Burpees Hybrid, Total Marketer,* downy and powdery mildew-resistant (Shumway). *Park's Comanche* and *Poinsett,* downy and powdery mildew-resistant (Parks). *Salty,* resistant to cucumber mosaic, powdery mildew and scab (Nichols)
EGGPLANT: *Faribo Hybrid,* disease-resistant (Farmers)

KALE: *Dwarf Blue Curled Vates,* withstands below freezing temperatures (Burpee)

LETTUCE: *Oakleaf,* hot weather-resistant. *Butter King, Bibb* or *Limestone,* hot weather-tolerant (Shumway). *Premier Great Lakes,* resistant to tip-burn and heat (Burpee)

MUSKMELON: *Edisto,* disease and mildew-resistant; *Mainerock,* wilt-resistant; *Saticoy,* powdery mildew and fruit spot-resistant (Parks). *Harvest Queen,* fusarium wilt-resistant (Farmers)

PEAS: *Early Alaska,* wilt-resistant. *American Wonder,* drought-resistant (Henry Fields). *Drought-Proof* (Burgess)

PEPPER: *Yolo Wonder,* tobacco mosaic-resistant (Gurney's)

RADISH: *Cherry Belle,* pithiness-resistant (Shumway)

SPINACH: *Hybrid No. 7,* resistant to downy mildew (Burpee)

SWEET CORN: *Golden Beauty,* disease-resistant. *Silver Queen,* disease-tolerant (Parks)

TOMATOES: *VF Tomato,* verticillium, fusarium wilt-resistant; *Sunray,* fusarium wilt-resistant (Burpee). *Sunset, Starfire,* sunscald-resistant; *Monte Carlo,* multiple disease-resistant (Farmers). *Crack-Proof* (Burgess)

TURNIP: *Tokyo Cross,* virus and other disease-resistant (Burpee)

WATERMELON: *Faribo Striped Giant Hybrid,* fusarium-resistant (Farmers). *Dixie Queen,* wilt-resistant (Burpee)

This by no means exhausts the lists of disease-resistant vegetables and more are constantly being developed. Note resistant strains when you check your seed catalogs. Many of the varieties listed here also are sold by other seed companies.

DNA. DNA is the hereditary material of the cell, and it is now well established that purified DNA (genetic material) can be taken up by bacteria and the receiving cells are able to incorporate it into their chromosomes and express the genes so acquired. Experiments by L. Ledoux and R. Huart, biochemists at the Center of Study of Nuclear Energy in Mol, Belgium, and M. Jacobs, a plant geneticist at the University of Brussels, have shown that thiamine deficiency in the flowering plant *Arabidopsis thaliana* can be corrected by bacterial DNA.

Some strains of this plant were unable to synthesize thiamine and were not able to grow and reproduce without supplements. The plants then were treated with bacterial DNA and they grew and reproduced without the thiamine supplements. Furthermore they were able to produce progeny that were not deficient in thiamine. It seems, therefore, that the bacterial DNA provided the plants with the necessary thiamine gene, and further that this genetic correction was inheritable by the next generation. Further experimentation in this area may prove very valuable in food plant development.

Dock (*Rumex crispus*).   Curled dock is both a food and a medicine. In the old days it was gathered to "thin and purify the blood" in the spring of the year. There is no evidence to support this claim, but the high vitamin C content of dock undoubtedly was beneficial, particularly after a winter diet deficient in greens. The greens also are richer in vitamin A than carrots.

Dock is good to calm the pain of stinging nettle. Crush the juicy leaves and rub on the affected area.

Drying Herbs.   Leaf herbs should be cut, washed, tied in loose bunches and allowed to drip dry. Place in large brown paper bags which have been labeled. Close the mouth of the bag about the

Dry herbs in paper bags hung in an airy place.

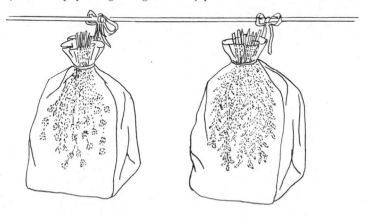

stems; let the herbs hang free inside the bag. Hang the bags where they will have good air circulation. Dried this way none of the oils is absorbed by contact with the paper as may be the case if dried herbs are stored in cardboard boxes.

With seed herbs, let the plants mature until the ripe seeds part from the dry umbels with a little pressure. This occurs after they lose their greenish color but before they will drop of their own accord. Cut the heads on a dry morning, spread them out on brown paper in the sun for the rest of the day, stirring occasionally. Do this for several days, taking them in at night, until thoroughly dry. Seeds may be stored in opaque glass bottles or clear ones away from the light.

Dusty Miller (*Cinerara*).   Plant this around prized flowers to repel rabbits and other animals. George W. Park, president of Park Seeds, gave me this suggestion and he believes *Cinerara Diamond* to be the most effective type, and the prettiest.

Dyers Greenwood (*Genista tinctoria*).   Once this was considered a very useful plant for dyeing. Bees like it for its honey and sheep and goats like to graze it, but it is thought that its bitter taste affects the milk of cows that eat it.

E

Eelgrass (*Zostera marina*).   Eelgrass is harvested in spring by the Seri Indians, according to botanist Felger of the University of Arizona, along the Gulf of California in Sonora, Mexico. It has an edible grain and is a widely distributed sea plant along the coasts of North America and Eurasia.

The upper stem fruits in the spring, then breaks off and floats on the surface of the water. The Seri harvest the grain when large quantities of the plant are found floating loose near the shore.

Eelgrass has a content of protein and starch similar to that of grains grown on land. Once it is dry, it is separated from the seaweed with which it grows, and the grains are toasted and ground into flour. Cooked into a gruel it may be eaten with honey. It is the only ocean plant known which has a grain used as a human food resource.

The Seri find many other uses for the eelgrass one of which is a cure for diarrhea. It is also piled over house frames for shade and made into toys for the children. Others find it makes an excellent mulch for garden or orchard.

Fresh-water eelgrass (*Hydrocharitaceae*, genus *Vallisneria*, species *americana*), also known as tapegrass and wild celery, grows in the mud of shallow ponds, sending up ribbonlike leaves directly from the root. (See SUPPLIERS INDEX.)

Eelworm. Eelworms or nematodes are tiny, sightless, eel-shaped organisms which pierce the roots of plants to feed or to lay their eggs inside causing knots to form. When organic matter is incorporated into the soil it encourages beneficial fungi and other nematodes which feed on the plant-parasitic variety of eelworms. These beneficial fungi grow in decomposing vegetable matter and kill the nematodes. It is possible to reduce wireworm and nematode attack, too, by placing a heavy dressing of barnyard manure on grassland before plowing.

Another aid in controlling nematodes is a legume, crotalaria. A predatory fungus, arthrobotrys, traps nematodes on small spherical knobs which sometimes are called "lethal lollipops." These are coated with a sticky substance which kills the nematodes on contact. They adhere without possibility of escape and are consumed by the fungus.

A member of this group, *Arthrobotrys oligospora Fres.*, has been used with success against the potato root eelworm. This fungus is generally found in soils rich in organic matter such as decaying vegetation or animal manure.

The genus *Mononchus* of soil-inhabiting predaceous nematodes also has attracted attention for a possible use against specific species of plant parasites. The *Mononchus papillatus* in particular, U.S.D.A. plant pathologist W. A. Feder found, controlled sugar beet nematodes.

thyme — good health
tarragon

not where tomatoes or eggplant last year
Black Magic Hybrid

Burpee's Early Beauty Hybrid

Eggplant (*Solanum melongena*).   Redroot pigweed makes egg-plant more resistant to insect attack. During dry weather, mulch-ing and irrigation will help to prevent wilt disease. Dry cayenne pepper sprinkled on plants while still wet with dew will repel caterpillars. Eggplant growing among green beans will be pro-tected from the Colorado potato beetle. The beetles like eggplant even more than potatoes, but they find the beans repellant.

Elderberry (*Sambucus nigra* and *Sambucus canadensis*).   Elder-berries, having a liking for moist soil, are helpful near compost yards that are difficult to drain, and will also assist in the fermen-tation of the compost. Elderberries are noted for their ability to produce very fine humus soil about their roots.

Elecampane (*Inula helenium*).   My German heritage bids me have great respect for elecampane, sometimes called horseheal or horse elder, because it was under the protection of the goddess Hulda, who first taught mortals the art of spinning and weaving flax. Candied elecampane, according to a 17th century herbal, was thought to "cause mirth."

Elecampane came to America as a healer, being introduced into gardens as a home remedy. Finding the climate congenial it went native and now grows wild in many places.

The substance most abundantly contained in elecampane root is *inulin,* a sort of invert starch usable as a replacement for ordi-nary starch in the diet of diabetics. It also contains a volatile oil and several identifiable crystalline substances. The thick, yellow taproot has the odor of camphor.

Elecampane once was used in England for the heaves in horses, and as far back as 1885 a Dr. Korab demonstrated that the active bitter principle of the plant, called *helenin* was a powerful anti-septic and bactericide, particularly destructive to the tubercle bacillus.

Elecampane in the garden provides a six-foot tall accent of bright yellow in midsummer when the large-rayed flowers stand above the enormous felty leaves. The plants are useful in providing a bit of shade for lower-growing mints.

Elements of Plants. It becomes easier to understand how and why plants affect each other when we know the many different elements of which they are composed.

Certain chemical elements are present in all living protoplasm, both plant and animal. Most abundant of these are oxygen, carbon, hydrogen and nitrogen, listed in order of abundance. These elements ordinarily constitute 95 to 98 percent of active, living protoplasm.

In addition other chemical elements in smaller quantities probably are always present (in green plants, at least). They are sulfur, zinc, boron, manganese, phosphorus, calcium, magnesium, iron, molybdenum copper and chlorine. In green plants all of these are physiologically significant and perform definite and very necessary functions.

Frequently chemical analyses show the presence in plant tissues of other elements such as nickel, gold, tin and mercury, some weeds having the ability to take up a great deal of gold. These elements apparently are not required in the physiology of plants and even may be toxic. They are found in the plants because they happen to be present in the soil where the plants grow, and the plants are unable to prevent their absorption.

Because of this fact, plants have been used to help locate deposits of valuable minerals such as uranium and selenium. One method involves the use of indicator plants—those that are known to tolerate the accumulation of abnormally large quantities of certain minerals. Another method involves the testing of many or all species in a given area by chemical analysis. In many instances "botanical prospecting" has proven very useful.

In the plant world plant excretions, drawn from the elements which make them up, are used as a protection against disease. The soil is structured and works in certain ways because of the effect of all the chemical elements that plants pump into the soil to protect their interests. Healthy plants can excrete larger quantities of these substances, which may be antibiotic or fungicidal. In a mixed planting these substances often are beneficial to other plants, while in a monoculture the build-up of certain elements may be very detrimental.

Elm *(Ulmus).* Grapevines that climb trees, swinging high in the air, are greatly benefited by good air circulation and sunlight. It is the sunlight on their leaves rather than on the grapes that causes them to ripen to perfection. Elm trees as supports for grapevines are particularly beneficial.

The slippery elm *(U. fulva)* is also known as the red elm and the moose elm because its wood is red, and moose are fond of browsing its young shoots. When the bark is stripped from this valuable tree it is possible to scrape from its inner surface the thick, fragrant, mucilaginous cambium—a delectable substance that allays both hunger and thirst. The inner bark, dried, ground and mixed with milk, is a valuable food for invalids. Fevers and acute inflammatory disorders have been treated with the bark, and poultices of the bark also relieve throat and chest ailments.

Esparsette *(Onobrychis viciaefolia).* This perennial forage legume of Eurasian origin also is called medick, sanfoin, lucifer, snail clover and great trefoil. The plant was introduced into England by the Romans, but it is not much grown today, possibly because it takes several years to reach fruition. It produces three crops a year however, and grows again from the same roots once it reaches maturity. Oddly enough in England the spike-like flowers are violet but in China they are yellow.

Esparsette is a good food for cattle and is equally nourishing for humans. It is valuable for those suffering from weight loss yet reduces weight in those who are too heavy. It is considered a tonic both for the brain and spinal cord. The roots of a variety called black medick make a good tooth powder.

Esparsette is recommended as a border plant for small grains or vegetables, and in a thin stand it aids growth of corn. It also may be grown as a lightly-scattered stand with small grains. The seed retains viability for up to three years, and grows well in limestone soils.

Essential Oils. These organic compounds which occur widely in plant tissues are often regarded as waste products of plant metabolism, but they are actually very important. Although called "oils" they are chemically different from true oils and fats, most of them being among the organic compounds called *terpenes*, which are made up of carbon and hydrogen only, with no oxygen.

The essential oils are aromatic substances that cause the odors and flavors characteristic of many plant parts, such as fragrant flowers, mint leaves, cinnamon bark, clove buds, sandalwood, nutmeg seeds and pine needles. Essential oils are important in medicine, food flavoring, perfumes, cosmetics and many other products.

These exudates from the roots, leaves or flowers also cause plants to be either protective or repellent to other plants growing near them, or to influence them in other ways. They also enable certain plants either to attract or repel insect life, or to be selective in attracting a certain type of insect. A curious plant, dictamnus (*burning bush*), has one species which gives off a volatile oil from the upper parts of its stems which may be ignited on hot days and which will burn without harming the plant.

Euphorbia (*Euphorbiaceae*).   A few well-placed plants of caper spurge (*E. lathyrus*) will deter moles and mice and thus, are good to plant near young fruit trees. Many of the spurge family like dry, light, sandy soils but will spread to cultivated land if given a chance. They all have a sharp, milky juice with some poisoning effect, and which in the leafy spurge. (*E. elsula*) and the cypress spurge have been used against warts.

F

Fennel (*Nigella sativa*).   Most plants dislike fennel and it is one herb which should be planted well away from the vegetable garden, since it has an inhibiting effect on bush beans, caraway, kohlrabi and tomatoes. Fennel planted away from the garden is valuable for its masses of fringed foliage. At one time the fragrant seeds, which smell and taste like licorice, were made into a tea soothing to colicky babies. Mixed with peppermint leaves it also makes a delicious tea for adults. Fennel is inhibited by the presence of coriander and will not form seed. It also dislikes wormwood.

Fern, Male (*Dryopteris filix-mas*). My beloved old *Pharmacopoeia of the United States of America*, Seventh Decennial Revision, 1890, speaks of this fern eloquently, referring to its taste as "sweetish, acrid, somewhat bitter, astringent and nauseous." It does not, however, say that fern seed will make you invisible as the "Doctrine of Signatures" once stated. That ferns have medicinal value has been recognized for centuries and they are still listed in the *Pharmacopoeia* today, the useful species including also the evergreen wood fern (*D. marginalis*). In the autumn the roots are carefully dug, cleaned and dried and the substance *oleoresin* is extracted through the use of ether.

Perhaps it is because of the oleoresin that ferns and beeches (*Fagus*) have an inhibiting effect on each other. However, a compost made of ferns assists tree seeding and is useful to tree nurseries to encourage germination.

Fertilizers, Nature's Own. We all are familiar with the nitrogen-fixing traits of legumes which draw nitrogen from the air and "fix" it on their roots. Actually there are many plants which get only about five percent of their nourishment directly from the soil. Have you ever noticed how plants, particularly grass, look greener after a thunderstorm? This is not an optical illusion. They really *are* greener as a result of the electrically-charged air which frees its 78 percent nitrogen content in a water-soluble form.

Rain and lightning are fertilizing agents. Each time lightning strikes the earth large amounts of nitrogen are charged into the ground. One authority states that 250,000 tons of natural nitrogen are produced every day in the 1,800 thunderstorms taking place somewhere on the earth. In some places this may amount to more than 100 pounds per acre per year. Rain also brings nitrogen—in some areas as much as 20 pounds per acre annually.

Sulfur comes down with the rain, possibly producing as much as 40 pounds per acre per year. Rain water also contains carbonic acid, forming carbon dioxide in the soil where it is needed for the plant-feeding relationship. Millions of tons fall yearly, and when we consider that nearly half the make-up of a plant is carbon we realize how important this is. Evidence also seems to show that rare minerals such as selenium and molybdenum are washed down in rain.

Snow, which furnishes not only nitrogen but phosphorus and other minerals, yields an extra bonus denied warm climate areas. Snow contains forty percent less *heavy water* or deuterium oxide, than normal water. Deuterium is a heavy isotope, a form of hydrogen but a little different. Combined with water it does not form H_2O, the water molecule, but D_2O instead. Heavy water, according to the Russian scientists who observed this, slows down some chemical and biological processes of growing plants. When the heavy water molecules are removed plants seem to grow faster. Thus crops are aided in short-season, snowy-climates such as Alaska. Even fog contributes to the soil's fertility, especially along the seacoast where it brings in large quantities of iodine, nitrogen and chlorine.

Dust, though sometimes disagreeable, has its good points too, containing minerals, organic matter and beneficial organisms often in substantial quantities essential to plant growth. Dust may be carried for thousands of miles, even being held suspended for long periods in the upper atmosphere to be washed down eventually by rain. Many believe that dust is one of the most significant factors in restoring minerals to the exhausted soil and that it also contains bacteria important to healthy soil life.

Here's a way you can obtain some of the benefits of electroculture without waiting for a thunderstorm. Tie your tomato plants to metal poles or trellises (we use concrete reinforcing wire bent in an inverted V-shape, with a row of tomato plants on each side), with nylon strips cut from discarded panty hose. These sturdy supports also attract static electricity. A friend who tried this reported that she not only harvested an abundant crop but they were extremely large tomatoes, and her plants continued producing right up to frost.

Feverfew (*Chrysanthemum parthenium*).   Sometimes this plant is called pyrethrum. It is not the same plant, but it has insect repellent properties of its own, perhaps because of the spicy scent of its foliage.

Flax (*Linum usitatissimum*).   Flax is a good companion to both carrots and potatoes, improving both their growth and flavor. Flax planted near potatoes will protect against the Colorado potato beetle. (See chapter on POISONOUS PLANTS.)

Leaf extracts of the false flax (*Camelina sativa* and *C. microcarpa*), frequently found growing in flax fields, have an inhibiting effect on flax itself.

Fleabane (*Erigeron*).   This is one of our native plants that has spread to Europe and has taken possession of stony soils. It is used for medicinal purposes, and the acrid oil as a mosquito repellent. But some people are allergic to this plant, reacting to it as they would to poison ivy.

Flea Beetle (*Faltica* and *Epitrix*).   Flying insects such as flea beetles are known to dislike moisture. Very often they can be discouraged by watering the garden in full sunlight. I find them annoying but not particularly destructive to eggplant, tomato, turnip and radish plants. The damage is mostly cosmetic, and strong plants quickly grow out of it, the plants becoming less attractive to the beetles as the leaves enlarge and toughen a little. Light cultivation and the addition of organic matter to the soil both discourage the beetles and help the plants.

Bruised elderberry leaves laid over the rows of plants is a deterrent to the beetles, and they also are repelled by mint or wormwood. Beetles attracted to radish or kohlrabi may be controlled by interplantings of lettuce.

Foxglove (*Digitalis*).   The very powerful drug digitalis is made from the dried leaves of the purple foxglove, one of our most delightful garden flowers. The derivative is valuable in treating neu-

Some people plant soybeans and corn as a lure or trap crop for deer; others plant castor beans and foxglove to repel them. An effective fence has to be at least seven feet high.

ralgia, asthma, palpitations of the heart and as a cardiac stimulant, to name but a few of its many uses.

British physician William Withering introduced digitalis in 1785 as a treatment for certain heart diseases. Off the record its discovery is credited to a Shropshire witch, who probably knew far more about its effects than did the English doctor. The drug is cumulative in its action and should never be used as a medication except under the direction of a physician. (See chapter on POISON-OUS PLANTS.)

Foxglove not only stimulates our hearts but has a beneficial effect on plants growing near it, particularly on pine trees. This is quite a natural association, since foxglove likes to grow on the borders of forests and open places in the woods. A tea made of foxglove will keep cut flowers fresh.

Freckles. I do not dislike freckles—my mother always told me they were the scars left by the angels' kisses—but some lucky people seem to receive more kisses than they want. If freckles trouble you, elderflowers added to facial steam baths will clear and soften the skin, and are also good against freckles and faulty pigmentation, especially when they are used in conjunction with whey and yoghurt. Such face packs not only are soothing but are tonic and stimulating. Parsley water externally used also is said to remove freckles or moles.

Freshly crushed leaves or freshly pressed juice of lady's mantle (*Alchemilla vulgaris*) is helpful against inflammation of the skin and acne, as well as freckles. Externally used lime flowers (*Tilia*) are a fine cosmetic against freckles, wrinkles and impurities of the skin, and they also are stimulating to hair growth.

People who spend a great deal of time in their gardens occasionally are subject to sunburn. Don't forget just how good aloe vera is for this as well as other burns.

French Intensive Gardening. This type of gardening, which stresses maximum use of the soil and first became popular in the 1800's, is largely accomplished by using raised beds which may be any length but are narrow enough to permit easy handling from either side.

Prepare the soil by loosening to a depth of 12 inches and removing all weeds. Add compost or well-decomposed manure as well as any other organic pH modifiers (agricultural lime, gypsum, bone meal, phosphate rock, etc.), which a soil test may indicate. Double digging is then done. This means that where the first spade-depth of soil is removed, a second spade-depth of soil is loosened before soil from the top layer is replaced.

If you are working with extremely poor soil the bottom spade-depth may need to have additional incorporations of sand, compost and loamy soil. All this sounds like a lot of work, and it is, but as the soil is improved each year the work gets easier.

The benefit derived from this intensive gardening method is the increased number of plants which may be grown close together in a very small area. Perhaps in no other form of gardening is

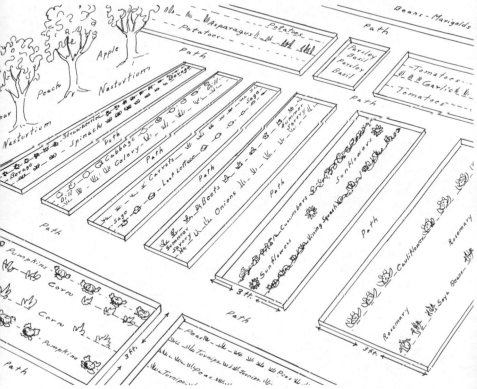

French Intensive Gardening method is an ideal way to save space and to use companion planting effectively.

companion planting so important, since herbs and vegetables are so closely crowded together.

Raised beds have the advantage of improved drainage and better aeration. The soil does not become waterlogged in winter and as a result it warms up faster in spring and produces earlier crops. In general the smaller vegetables and salad greens are best suited to this type of culture but there is no law that says you can't grow corn and pumpkins and sunflowers and cucumbers this way if you want to!

Frost.   Vegetables frequently are classified according to their ability to survive frosts. The U.S. Department of Agriculture defines the differences:

Hardy or cool-season crops will survive medium to heavy frosts. Seed from this group (peas, beets, kale, etc.), can be planted as soon as the soil can be prepared in the spring or in midsummer for a late fall crop.

Semi-hardy vegetables will survive a light frost. Seed will germinate at relatively low temperatures, and can be planted 2 to 3 weeks before the last frost date. This necessarily will vary in different sections of the country.

Tender or warm season crops (tomatoes, eggplant, bell peppers, etc.) are injured or killed by frost, and their seeds seldom germinate in cold soil.

Fruit Trees.   Fruit trees benefit from an interplanting of 15 percent mustard with clovers. Other good companion plants are chives, garlic, onions, nasturtiums, horseradish, southernwood and stinging nettle.

Nut trees usually take a little longer to bear than fruit trees. While you are waiting for them to grow, interplant with peanuts (legumes). They will improve the soil and give you a crop as well. (See chapter on POLLINATION COMPANIONS.)

Fumigation.   Greenhouse gardeners, who frequently have difficulty controlling aphids, ants and termites as well as that all-time pest, white fly, find smoke from oak leaves effective. They are not poisonous, do not kill soil bacteria and leave no harmful residue. Smoke the leaves for about a half hour, keeping the greenhouse door tightly closed.

Fungi.   Fungi are plants without chlorophyll—some are very useful and even edible, others very troublesome.

Mushrooms are edible fungi (the non-poisonous types), which have a natural affinity for plants in woods, fields and meadows. The part of the mushroom we see is just a small portion of the entire plant. Most of it is underground, a tangled, twisted jungle of threads that forms the mycelium. The mushroom itself is the reproductive part of the plant, the fruiting body, which under the right conditions of moisture and temperature grows easily.

My sister-in-law in Missouri once brought home some morels from her father's farm and took them outdoors to her backyard to trim. She threw the pan of trimmings under an apple tree in her small orchard and was surprised sometime later to find morels growing thriftily there. They continued to come up intermittently for several years.

The delicious morels are fairly common in the United States. The fruiting body, like that of other mushrooms, grows above the ground and resembles a sponge. Because of this they are easy to identify and safe for the collector to gather for the table. They are often found in apple orchards just about the time the trees are blossoming.

Truffles are another type of fungi, but they grow several inches

The distinctive morel mushroom is especially delicious, often is found growing in apple orchards about the time the trees bloom.

Morchella elata

Morchella semilbera

below the ground and are not visible. They are rare in the United States but are quite common in Spain, England, Italy and France where they grow under oak and chestnut trees. Here they are found by dogs and pigs specially trained to locate them by smell. Should you see a French farmer following a pig on a leash this is simply a routine way of picking truffles, which sell for fantastic prices.

Because of their close association with oak and chestnut trees, scientists believe, the truffles help the tree roots assimilate chemicals from the soil. Truffles vary from 1/4th inch to 4 inches in diameter and resemble an acorn, a walnut, or a potato. The spores are borne within the tuberlike body of the fungus. They have a delicious taste and serve as a condiment. They are black and thus very attractive as a garnish for salads.

Fungus on tree roots first was reported in 1885 by the German botanist A. B. Frank. His belief that water and nutrients were entering the tree through the fungus was scoffed at, but we know today that the fungus acts as a link between the soil and the rootlets of the plant. The tree in turn helps the mycorrhizal fungus by providing root metabolites, substances which are vital to the fungus for the completion of its full life cycle.

Many mushrooms are deadly poison and no one who is inexperienced should ever gather them for food. The deadly amanita, sometimes called the "destroying angel" can cause death in less than six hours. Yet many of the poisonous mushrooms also serve a purpose in promoting healthy growth in other plants.

Mildews are a type of fungi which can be extremely troublesome and difficult to control when they form on plants, usually due to combined moisture and humidity. They attack grapes, lettuce, tomatoes, roses, peas, tobacco, potatoes, cucumbers and many other fruits and vegetables, usually forming a gray or white, powderlike coating on the surface of the leaves. I have found that it is possible to partly control this fungus with a dusting of wettable sulphur. Sunshine and good air circulation is the best remedy.

Smut is a fungus that attacks such grains as wheat, barley, rye, corn and oats. It looks like a large sac or tumor among the kernels when it appears on an ear of corn. The sac contains a large mass of black spores.

Smuts act on the host plant in a different way from most parasitic fungi. The mycelium that grows among the cells of the host stimulates them to produce a swelling or gall. The spores develop as a black mass within the gall and are thrown into the air when the gall breaks.

Smuts are difficult to control as, unlike the spores of any other fungi that attach themselves to the seed, these lie dormant in the ground through the winter. In the spring new kinds of spores are germinated and reinfect the corn plants. Treating the seed is seldom effective in preventing corn smut. The best answer seems to be crop rotation and the development and use of strains of corn that are smut-resistant.

G

Garlic (*Allium sativum*).   Eldon L. Reeves and S. V. Amonkar of the University of California discovered garlic to be a powerful destroyer of mosquitoes, achieving a 100 percent kill of five species of California mosquito larvae by spraying breeding ponds with a garlic-based oil.

Monsignor David Greenstock of The Henry Doubleday Research Association in England found that an oil of garlic emulsion used as an insecticide killed 89 percent of aphids and 95 percent of onion flies.

Greenstock also fed garlic to chickens, mice and rabbits and found that it actually improved their health. He found further that the active principle of garlic, *allicin,* is a complex mixture of substances which are mainly allyl sulfides. These are produced by enzyme activity in the bulb, where their balance and effectiveness are dependent upon the presence of assimilable sulphur. This sulphur is produced in the soil by a number of microorganisms, principally certain tiny fungi that are unable to grow without the presence of humus. Organically-grown garlic, then, is believed to be most effective, because that grown with chemical fertilizers does not have enough humus to support the fungi.

Grow your own garlic and try this recipe. Take 3 to 4 ounces of chopped garlic bulbs and soak in 2 tablespoons of mineral oil for one day. Add a pint of water in which one teaspoon fish emulsion has been dissolved. Stir well. Strain the liquid and store in a glass or china container, as it reacts with metals. Dilute this, starting with 1 part to 20 parts of water and use as a spray against your worst insect pests. If sweet potatoes or other garden plants are attracting rabbits try this spray. Rabbits dislike the smell of fish, too. Garlic sprays are useful in controlling late blight on tomatoes and potatoes.

Garlic grown in a circle around fruit trees is good against borers. It is beneficial to the growth of vetch and is protective planted with roses and also good against grain weevils, when the cloves are stored in the grain. All alliums, however, inhibit the growth of peas and beans. Plant garlic with tomatoes against red spider. I have done this for three successive years with good results.

The Babylonians and Hindus knew of garlic's medicinal powers 3,000 years ago, and it was well known to the ancient Egyptians, who fed great quantities of garlic to the slaves who built the pyramids. The Greek physicians, fathers of present-day medicine, used garlic in their prescriptions, and it was rationed to the soldiers of the mighty Roman armies.

The 800-year-old medical school of Salerno included garlic in their *materia medica,* and it always has been one of the standbys of folk medicine practitioners.

Garlic, Meadow (*Allium vineale*).   Meadow garlic's very penetrating taste and odor give a bad taste to milk if eaten by cows (see Cows), and the bulblets in wheat will spoil the flour. It's hard to eradicate because the little bulbs grow deeper and deeper into the soil with the passing years. If pastures or fields are badly infested, crop rotation is recommended.

But even wild garlic has a definite health value, and medicines derived from it are of value against high blood pressure and sclerosis.

Geranium (*Pelargonium*). Geraniums will repel cabbage worms and are good to plant among roses, grapes and corn against Japanese beetles. Use the white variety near corn.

Among the diverse scented geraniums are the peppermint geranium (*P. tomentosum*), which has velvety, grape-like leaves and small white blossoms; the lemon-scented (*P. crispum*), with long-stemmed, conspicuous flowers of a deep rose color and crispy, fruit-fragrant leaves; and nutmeg and apple geraniums which have small, almost rounded, soft gray leaves distinguished by the scent of spice or apple. Try making apple jelly flavored with rose geranium leaves.

Germination. Many plants not only inhibit the seed germination of other plants but their own as well. Experiments with western ragweed (*Ambrosia psilostachya*) by Robert L. Neill and Elroy L. Rice of the University of Oklahoma show that it is inhibitory to nitrogen-fixing algae and bacteria as well as to nitrifying bacteria.

Field studies indicated a different pattern of vegetation around the ragweed, and that these patterns are due neither to mineral nor physical properties of the soil nor to competition. It is the root exudate, leaf leachate and decaying leaves of the ragweed that inhibit many of the early invaders of abandoned fields.

The root exudates from rye grass and wheat seedlings suppress germination of seeds of field or corn camomile, the scentless camomile or corn mayweed. Bean seedlings suppress germination of wheat or flax seeds. Violets suppress wheat seedlings, too.

In some plants the suppressing substances may be formed in the seeds and fruits, in others in the roots, leaves or stems. Essential oils in many herbs, and even in trees such as poplar, citrus or the conifers, inhibit the germination of seeds of other plants to varying degrees.

Ginseng (*Panax quinquefolium*). Wild ginseng needs the companionship of trees to provide the filtered sunlight it requires to grow. When raised in beds for commercial use it is covered with lattice-work to protect it from the heat of the sun which would kill it. The Chinese believe that ginseng will cure nearly every disease, yet even now Western science is not sure whether it has real value or not. Physicians regard its benefits as largely psychological but tests in the Soviet Union and elsewhere indicate that infusions of the root actually may increase energy and resistance to infection.

Gladiolus (*Gladiolus*).   Peas, beans and gladiolus have inhibiting effects on each other.

Goldenrod (*Solidago*).   There are more than 60 native species of goldenrods, some growing on dry soil low in humus, others on soil that is rich and moist. If you would eliminate the goldenrod, cut it before it goes to seed and improve your soil with organic matter and better crops.

Gopher (*Geomyidae*).   These burrowing rodents may be repelled by plantings of scilla bulbs. The scillas, sometimes called squills, are flowering, bulb-like ornamentals which have grass-like leaves and clusters of flowers at the top of long stems. They are easy to grow and bloom in the early spring. They may be grown among vegetables as well as in flower beds. But be cautious—the bulbs should never be eaten.

Grapevine (*Vitis* and *Muscadina*).   (See chapter on POLLINATION.)

Grass, Crab (*Digitaria sanguinalis*).   Crab grass is one of the most troublesome lawn pests. Handpulling is recommended on lawns (before they form a mat), and much and frequent cultivation in gardens. As with Bermuda, dry hot weather will wilt the roots if they are brought to the surface. (See also QUACK GRASS.)

Grasses, Lawn.   Bermuda Grass (*Cynodon dactylon*) is an excellent lawn grass for the southern states. Bermuda withstands both heat and drought and will grow reasonably well even on poor soils. It may be started by seeding or sodding.

Never allow Bermuda to get started in the garden or flower beds, for it spreads quickly on cultivated soil, competing with flowers or vegetables for moisture. It may be killed out in the summer by hoeing and exposing the rhizomes to hot sunlight.

PAMPAS (*Cortaderia*). This ornamental grass, best grown in the South, produces beautiful flower plumes which, if cut when fully developed, are useful for decorative purposes indoors during the winter. It is increased by root division, and it grows well as a specimen plant in the lawn.

KENTUCKY BLUE GRASS (*Poa*), an excellent grass for the North and East. It needs a quick-germinating and quick-growing grass, such as redtop, planted with it to provide a rapid ground cover to help crowd out weeds during its early development. After it gets a good start the blue grass will crowd out the nurse grass.

ST. AUGUSTINE (*Stenotaphrum secundatum*) also thrives in the South, being particularly good under trees or in other shady areas where Bermuda will not do well. It forms a thick mat and smothers weeds.

ZOYSIA (*Zoysia*) in cultivated species form dense turf and are very valuable for planting on sandy soils, especially in the South. It is propagated vegetatively by means of small pieces of turf called plugs. Zoysia will choke out crab grass and weeds.

Grasses, Pasture. With the development of the new "beefalo" hybrid cattle by D. C. Basolo of Tracy, California, rich pasture grasses suitable for grazing livestock take on even greater importance. The Beefalo, which is 3/8 buffalo, 3/8 Charolais and 1/4 Hereford, can be produced more economically than other breeds because it gains weight faster and can finish out on grass rather than grain.

Another breed, an old-timer attracting renewed attention, is the Texas Longhorn. This breed, though not as tasty as the Beefalo which is fine eating, also will finish out on grass.

BERMUDA, a very persistent and nutritious grass of the Southern United States, is useful for both pasture and lawn.

BUFFALO GRASS which grows on the Western ranges where bison used to graze, still serves as food for herds of cattle. It is also useful for binding the soil, preventing erosion.

GRAMA GRASS, occurring mostly in the Great Plains area, is excellent forage for livestock. It is widely used also in conservation to prevent soil erosion.

JOHNSON GRASS grows wild all over the Southwest and is often a great pest in gardens. Yet in pastures it is very nutritious for cattle to feed on.

ORCHARD GRASS growing under fruit trees suppresses in some degree the root growth of pears and apples. Rye grass is often grown in nut orchards and serves as food for cattle which are allowed to graze and fertilize the land, from which they are removed at harvest time.

TEOSINTE, an annual grass often used as fodder for livestock, is considered the nearest relative to maize or Indian corn of all the wild grasses. It grows wild in moist soil from Connecticut west to Kansas and south to Florida and Texas.

Sugar cane and bamboo are both giant grasses, while the great cereals of the world, grasses too, are wheat, corn, oats, rye, barley and rice. The main forage crops include alfalfa, bent, brome grass, buckwheat, clover, fescue, timothy and vetch. Wild grasses not previously listed include bluegrass, esparto, reed, sandbur, Sudan grass and wild barley.

Many grains and grasses, such as vetch and oats, or wheat and maize, grow well planted together, the growth of both being enhanced and increased. Grass suppresses the growth of sunflower.

Grasshopper (*Tettigoniidae* and *Locustidae*).   Grasshoppers are very difficult to control, especially where they come in from surrounding fields, but this spray will help: Grind together 2 to 4 hot peppers, 1 mild green pepper, 1 small onion and add one quart water. Let stand 24 hours and strain. This mixture also is good against aphids.

During times of grasshopper infestation an after-harvest plowing will discourage egg-laying, while spring tilling before seeding will prevent grasshoppers from emerging from the eggs still present. Extracts of chinaberry have proven useful, while sabidilla dust or extract is effective against these and many other insects.

Grasshoppers can be attracted by this bait: Fill several two-quart mason jars with a 10 percent molasses solution and place around the area where the infestation is the worst. Grasshoppers will eat almost anything except horehound but grasshopper-resistant varieties of corn and wheat have been developed.

Chickens are of great value in an orchard, for they eat grasshoppers and other insects and at the same time add their manure to aid the fertility of the soil. The coop may be moved every few days to a new location.

Wild birds attracted to the garden eat a great many grasshoppers and surprisingly cats will kill and eat them, too. I think this is partly for the fun they get out of the chase.

Green Manures.   Vegetable matter in the form of green manure is an extremely valuable additive to the soil. In an Hawaiian experiment, fresh green plant matter mixed with the soil resulted in a definite increase in the number of harmless free-living eelworms. As a further result a greater number of predaceous fungi occurred, causing a reduction in the population of the harmful eelworms or nematodes.

Green manures are cover crops usually achieved by planting low-priced seed which protects the soil surfaces of fields or garden plots from erosion from winter winds, snowstorms and quick thaws. It acts as an insulating blanket, keeping the soil warmer in winter and cooler in summer. This encourages soil life activity in general and earthworms in particular. The more earthworms in the soil, the more channels they'll burrow deep in the subsoil, bringing to the surface useful minerals and nutrients which will increase the health and insect-resistance of food plants.

The roots of many green manure crops themselves reach deeply into the subsoil where they, also, absorb and bring up valuable nutrients which will revitalize the soil when they are plowed under to decompose.

Certain green manure crops, the legumes, have the ability to capture and fix large amounts of nitrogen from the air, also adding this important plant food to the soil. Alfalfa is one of the best of these, and it is also high in terms of protein, which breaks down into usable nitrate fertilizer.

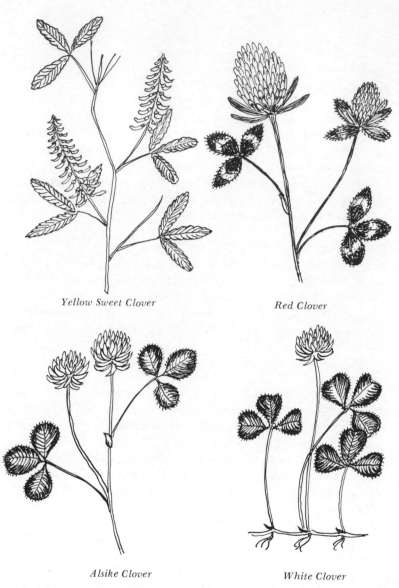

Yellow Sweet Clover

Red Clover

Alsike Clover

White Clover

The clovers make fine green manure crops. Its growth is limited by hen-bane and buttercup family members. It stimulates the growth of deadly nightshade.

Other useful green manure cover crops are barley, brome grass, buckwheat, cheat grass, alsike clover, cowpeas, lespediza, millet, rape, spring rye, Italian ryegrass, winter rye, sorghum, soybeans, Sudan grass, sunflowers, common clovers, hairy vetch and winter wheat.

For the home garden kale makes a good, thick non-leguminous green manure cover crop for the winter months. It is easy to grow, a tasty food with a flavor that is improved by frost, and you can actually dig it out from under the snow in the dead of winter. When the kale starts growing again in the spring it can be tilled under to add green manure to the soil for the spring garden.

H

Hazelnut (*Corylus*). In ancient times many believed that a forked hazel twig had supernatural powers. Such twigs are mentioned in the Bible, while the Romans also described the magical quality of the branches and told of hazel divining rods being used to find water or precious minerals underground.

Hazels furnish valuable cover and food for wildlife. People also plant them as ornamentals or to shelter other plants. In some forests hazels form such dense thickets that tree seedlings cannot grow and heavy machinery is needed to uproot them so more valuable timber can be planted.

Hazel trees and bushes are beneficial in pastures and elsewhere against flies. Cows also like to nibble on the leaves, which increase the butterfat in their milk, while the tannic acid also acts as a cleansing agent for their digestive systems.

Hedges. Hedges used as windbreaks are of particular value in dry, windy areas. Blueberries make a delightful hedge where they can be grown. Rosa rugosa makes an almost impenetrable hedge and also affords a harvest of vitamin-rich rose hips. Cardinal autumn olive (*Elaeagnus umbellata, Cardinal*) and dwarf burning bush (*Euonymus alatus compactus*) are beloved by birds, as is red-leaf barberry (*Berberis thumbergi atropurpurea*). For brilliant color there are Golden Prince euonymus (*Euonymus fortunei*) and Goldflame spirea (*Spirea bumalda*).

Hemp (*Cannabis sativa*).   It was not unusual in Holland in the 1800s to see a border of hemp planted around a cabbage field to keep white cabbage butterflies away. Hemp, we now know, has a protective effect on plants grown near it because the volatile substances it excretes inhibit the growth of certain pathogenic microorganisms. It is unlawful now, at least where I live, to grow hemp or marijuana. Check with your County Agent to find out if you can grow it.

Henbane (*Hyoscyamus niger, L.*).   Henbane like hemp is an ancient narcotic once used to treat disease, but which escaped to become naturalized in some parts of the country. The drug *hyoscyamine,* used to dilate the pupils of the eyes, is made from black henbane.

This poisonous herb is fatal to fowls, hence its name "henbane." All parts of the plant contain poisonous alkaloids, and even hogs sometimes are killed by eating its fleshy roots.

Herbs.   In his *The Life of the Forest* Jack McCormick gives this definition of herbs: "According to technical usage, *herbs* are not merely the aromatic plants used in cooking but any green plants that have soft rather than wood stems. Most wild flowers and grasses are herbs."

In her *Elixirs of Life* Mrs. C. F. Leyel considers as herbs agar-agar (*Plocaria lichenoides*), birds' nests (*Plocaria tenax*), bombax (*Bombas malabaricum*), cassava (*Jatropha manihot*), gold of pleasure (*Camelina sativa*) and hydrocotyle (*Hydrocotyle vulgaris*), along with dozens of other plants found in all parts of the world —the list is almost endless.

Herbs serve as both food and medicine and also in many instances as insect repellents. They aid or inhibit each other when grown in the vegetable garden or among flowers. In this book those that are most useful and most often found in our gardens, are treated separately, so I will not go into greater detail here. (See chapter on POISONOUS PLANTS.)

Herbs for Tea. Herb teas have both aided the digestions and given pleasure to untold generations. The herbs most frequently used are spearmint, peppermint, horsemint, Oswego tea, gill-over-the-ground, wintergreen, sassafras and catnip. Here is how to make tea:

Pick some of the leaves, using only those undamaged (but dried leaves may be used or, in the case of sassafras, the bark). You will need four or five leaves for a cup of tea and about a handful for a pot. Wash the leaves in cool water. Put in cup or pot and pour boiling water over them. Let steep, covered, for three to five minutes. Add sugar or honey to sweeten.

High-Vitamin Vegetables. A new tomato, *Doublerich,* introduced in 1956, contains as much vitamin C as citrus fruit. Prof. A. F. Yeager of the University of New Hampshire used crosses of the tiny wild Peruvian tomato, which is four times richer in vitamin C than our ordinary garden types.

A few years later *Caro-Red,* containing about 10 times the amount of vitamin A found in standard varieties, was perfected at the Indiana Experiment Station. *Caro-Red* owes its richness to its orange pigment, beta-carotene, and a single fruit will supply up to twice the minimum daily requirement of vitamin A for an adult. Perhaps best of all this is a very delicious tomato to eat. Still newer is *Caro-Rich,* which is reported to have even more vitamin A.

In 1958 the Oklahoma Experiment Station developed a sweet potato called *Allgold* with three times as much vitamin A and 50 percent more vitamin C than the commonly grown *Puerto Rico.*

A University of New Hampshire origination, *Sweetnut squash,* has a rich, nutlike flavor, edible seeds and contains 35 percent protein and 35 to 40 percent unsaturated oils. The hull-less seeds can be readily dried and eaten. New Hampshire also brought out the *Sweetheart* beet, 50 percent sweeter than any standard table variety and also containing more solids.

Strawberry varieties considered richest in vitamin C include *Beacon, Catskill, Fairfax, Fairpeake, Dresden, Sparkle, Midland, Premier* and *Tennessee Beauty,* among the June bearers. *Mastadon, Robinson* and *Gem* are the best among the everbearers.

The average blueberry type contains about 20 milligrams of vitamin C per hundred grams of fruit, but *Burlington, June* and *Rubel* test much higher. In the large fruiting varieties *Blue Ray* has the highest vitamin C content.

Potatoes do not contain as much vitamin C as many fruits, but those that test highest are *Katahdin, Irish Cobbler* and *Kennebec.* Apples testing highest in C are *Baldwin, Northern Spy, Winesap* and *Yellow Newton.*

Honeybees (*Apis mellifera*).   Both in the garden and in the orchard honeybees are an important agent of pollination. They are particularly attracted to the often inconspicuous flowers of herb plants.

A hive of bees is a good weather indicator, for if drones are forced out of the hive during fair weather it is a sign that cold, wet weather is imminent.

When hiving a new swarm of bees, rub the hive's inside with lemon balm, which the bees like. A smoke from jimson weed (datura) calms the bees when a hive is opened.

Horehound (*Marrubian vulgare*). In centuries past virtues attri-
buted to horehound included a cure for snakebite, and merit as a
fly repellent, vermifuge and as an ointment for wounds and itches.
The Hebrew name for the plant "Marrob" means a bitter juice.
It was one of the five bitter herbs required to be eaten at the Pass-
over Feast. The Romans considered it a good, and sometimes
magical herb. Horehound's real value relates to pulmonary ailments and it is widely used as an ingredient in lozenges for coughs
and colds.

For small stems and better quality grow close together the plants
intended for candymaking. Either the fresh or dried herb can be
used for this purpose.

Grasshoppers and other insects dislike the taste of horehound.
The plant grows well with tomatoes, improving their quality,
causing them to bear more abundantly and continue later in the
season.

Horseradish (*Ammoracia rusticana*). Horseradish and potatoes
have a symbiotic effect on each other, causing the potatoes to be
healthier and more resistant to disease. Plants should be set at the
corners of the potato plot only and should be dug after each season to prevent spreading. Horseradish does not seem to protect
against the potato beetle but it is effective against the blister beetle.
A tea made from horseradish is beneficial against monilia on apple
trees.

Horsetail (*Equisetum arvense L.*). The horsetails are the last remainder of the huge trees of the Carboniferous forests, and the
most common is the field horsetail which grows in sandy and gravelly soils on a high ground-water level.

This is a healing herb whose many uses have not received proper
attention. Made into a spray it is particularly useful against powdery fungus and curly leaf on peach trees. It also controls mildew
on roses, vegetables, grapes and stone fruits (see also MILDEW,
POWDERY), and has been found to have a cell-strengthening action
on the plants sprayed with it.

The parts used are the *dried* leaves and stems of the sterile form.

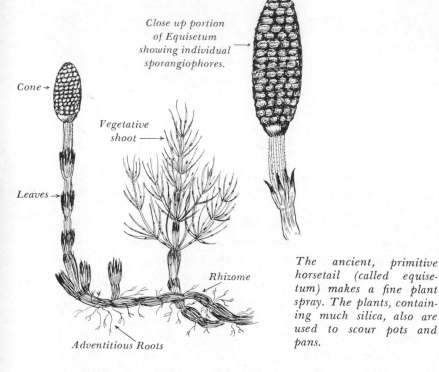

Close up portion of Equisetum showing individual sporangiophores. →

Cone →

Vegetative shoot ——→

Leaves →

Rhizome

Adventitious Roots

The ancient, primitive horsetail (called equise-tum) makes a fine plant spray. The plants, contain-ing much silica, also are used to scour pots and pans.

Boil two or three teaspoons of the crumbled herb to a cup of water for 20 minutes. Or soak the leaves in water for several hours, boil for 10 minutes and allow it to steep for another 10.

Horsetail looks like a tiny Christmas tree and sometimes is called the meadow pine. The hollow-branched, jointed stems range from 1 to 3 feet tall. The plant does not produce flowers or seeds but sends up fertile sporebearing stems resembling catkins. These are covered with powdery brown spores. After the spores drop, small green shoots emerge from the ground. The perennial horse-tail has a root stock which bears tuberous growths that store avail-able carbohydrates against a future need. The green shoots of horsetail contain a high percentage of silica, the controlling fac-tor against fungus diseases. If the green stems are burned in a hot but quiet flame, removing all organic parts, the white skeleton of silica which is left will show the original structure of the little stems.

While horsetail itself will stop external bleeding, a horsetail brew also may be used as a healing agent for abscesses, burns, cuts and scratches, for both animals and humans. Place a good handful of the dried leaves and stems in a stewpan with just enough vinegar (5 percent acidity) to cover. Simmer for no longer than 20 minutes, cool and strain. Keep in refrigerator. When needed for use, add one part brew to two parts cow or goat milk. Return any not needed to refrigerator. Horsetail brew is stingless, soothing and gentle in its action. A plastic squeeze bottle may be used for convenient application.

Nelson Coon in his *Using Plants for Healing* reports that horsetail contains some unknown factor which is poisonous to animals, indicating caution in using it medicinally.

Horsetails have still another use: Their high silica content makes them effective as "scouring brushes" for pots and pans, and campers still find them usually available and convenient for this purpose.

Hyssop (*Hyssopus officinalis*).   It's hard to find anything more delightful than a hyssop hedge in full sun. The blue, white and pink flowered hyssop grown with gray Roman wormwood makes an intriguing design. Hyssop leaves have a peculiar fragrance reminiscent of civet, yet some use them the same way as savory.

Sow the hyssop seeds in late fall so they will germinate first thing in the spring. Planted near grapevines they will increase their yield, and near cabbages will lure away the cabbage butterfly.

A compress of hyssop leaves is good for removing black and blue spots from bruises. Bees are very fond of visiting hyssop blossoms, yet many other insects find the plant repellent. Radishes will not do well if hyssop is nearby.

This is another of the bitter herbs used in Jewish ceremonies but it is not the true hyssop of the Bible, which is believed to be a species of origanum.

I

Ichneumonid Wasp (*Campoletis perdistinctus*). This wasp has been found by the Brownsville Experiment Station in Texas to parasitize at least 27 destructive species of moths and butterflies, but it *prefers* to deposit its eggs in bollworms and tobacco budworms.

Inoculants. Sold under various names such as "Legume Aid" (*Burpee*) and "Nitragen" (*Farmers*), this preparation is an aid to peas, beans, soybeans, sweet peas, etc. for better blooms and increased yields. Treating legume seeds with the inoculants helps them to develop nodules on their roots, which convert free nitrogen into plant food.

Insecticides. PLANTS. Garlic is an effective destroyer of the diseases that damage stone fruits, cucumbers, radishes, spinach, beans, nuts and tomatoes. Onion spray is effective as a non-toxic fumigant. A chemical from asparagus juice is an effective killer of nematodes such as root-knot sting, stubby root and meadow nematodes, and it is protective to tomatoes both on the roots and sprayed on the leaves. Harmless tree fungi called saprophytes help trees to resist such diseases as bark canker, decay fungi and leaf rust fungus.

PLANTS, AS ATTRACTANTS. Insects are largely attracted by scent and may be lured away from certain crops by other plants placed nearby. Plants such as nasturtium and mustard, both of which contain mustard oil, frequently are used for this purpose. These are called "trap crops." Insects feed on and lay their eggs in trap crops which should be destroyed before the eggs hatch.

PLANTS, AS REPELLANTS. Insect repellants may be prepared from crushed leaves, infusions or essential oils of such botanicals as citronella, eucalyptus, pennyroyal, bergamot, cedarwood, clove, rose geranium, thyme, wintergreen, lavender, cassia anise, sassafras, bay laurel or pine tar. Ginkgo, elder, pyrethrum and lavender repel ticks or other insects. Other plants such as cedar, quassia and teakwood themselves are immune to insects.

Insect-Resistant Vegetables and Grains.   Every garden has both "good" and "bad" bugs, yet from a gardener's point of view only a few are relatively destructive. Some vegetables seem to have a natural, built-in resistance: carrots, beets, endive (including escarolle and witloof chicory), chives, okra, Egyptian onions, parsley, peppers and rhubarb. Under good growing conditions lettuce might be added to this list, too.

Numerous vegetables and herbs listed in this book help other vegetables to resist insects when grown with or near them. Scientists have done a great deal of research, also, on why certain other plants are attractive to insects. They have come up with something that organic gardeners knew all along: insects prefer to eat plants having high concentrations of free amino acids, such concentrations being enhanced if the plants are improperly nourished. Organically-grown vegetables produced on balanced, healthy soils have significantly lower levels of free amino acids in their tissues than plants grown where chemical fertilizers have destroyed the balance. Such "organic" vegetables are less tasty to insects.

In his *Insect Resistance in Crop Plants* Reginald H. Painter, professor of entomology at the University of Kansas, gives excellent insight into the "why" of insect resistance. Here briefly are some of the conclusions researched from Mr. Painter's book and those of other writers:

PLANT	INSECT	VARIETIES		
		Resistant	Tolerant	Susceptible
Alfalfa	Spotted alfalfa aphid	*Cody* *Lahontan* *Zia*		*Buffalo*
Barley	Greenbugs	*Omugi* *Dictoo* *Will*		*Rogers*

PLANT	INSECT	VARIETIES		
		Resistant	Tolerant	Susceptible
Cabbage	Cabbage looper and imported cabbage worm	*Savoy Chieftan* *Red Acre* *Mammoth Rock Red* *Ferry's Hollander*		*Golden Acre*
Corn	Corn earworm	*Dixie 18* Field Corn *Calumet* Sweet Corn		
Cucumbers	Striped and spotted cucumber beetle	*Stono* (**moderately**) *Fletcher* *Niagara*		
Muskmelon	Striped and spotted cucumber beetle	*Hearts of Gold*		*Smith Perfect* *Crenshaw*
Potato	Colorado potato beetle	*Sequoia*		
	Aphids	*British Queen* *DeSota* *Early Pinkeye* *Houma* *Irish Daisy* *LaSalle*	*Red Warba* *Triumf* *President* *Peach Blow* *Early Rose*	*Katahdin* *Irish Cobbler* *Idaho Russet* *Sebago* *Sequoia*
Squash	Squash bug	*Butternut* *Table Queen* *Royal Acorn* *Sweet Cheese* *Early Golden Bush Scallop* *Early Summer Crookneck* *Early Prolific Straightneck* *Improved Green Hubbard*		*Striped Green Cushaw* *Pink Banana* *Black Zucchini*
	Striped and spotted cucumber beetle	*Royal Acorn* *Early Golden Bush Scallop*		*Caserta* *Black Zucchini*
Wheat	White stem sawfly	*Rescue* *Chinook*		*Tenmarq* *Bison*

PLANT	INSECT	VARIETIES		
		Resistant	Tolerant	Susceptible
		Ottawa		*Turkey*
		Ponca		*Kharkoff*
		Pawnee		*Kanred*
		Big Club 43		*Oro*
		Dual		*Cheyenne*
		Russell		*Minturki*
		Todd		*Zimmerman*
		Dawson		
		Honor		
		Illini Chief		
		Fulhard		
		Red Rock		
		Michigan Wonder		
	Hessian fly	**moderately resistant**		
		Blackhull		
		Superhard		
		Early Blackhull		
		Harvest Queen		
		Red Winter		
		Fulcaster		

Insects, Control of by Companion Planting.   Legumes planted in a rotation will protect grain crops and grasses from white grubs and corn rootworm. Chinch bug on corn and flea beetles are controlled by growing soybeans to shade bases of the plants. Worms in goats may be relieved by feeding them carrots, in horses by feeding mulberry leaves.

The following herbs may be planted as specific controls:

BASIL: Against flies and mosquitoes
BORAGE: Against tomato worm
CASTOR BEAN: Against moles and plant lice
CATNIP: Against flea beetles
DATURA: Against Japanese beetles
DEAD NETTLE: Against potato bugs
FLAX: Against potato bugs
GARLIC: Against Japanese beetle, aphis, weevils, fruit tree borers, spider mites

HENBIT: General insect repellent

HORSERADISH: Against potato bugs (plant at corners of plot)

HYSSOP: Against cabbage moth

LAVENDER: Against clothes moths (dry and place in garments)

MARIGOLDS: Against Mexican bean beetles, nematodes and many other insects

MINT: Against white cabbage moths, dried against clothes moths

MOLE PLANT: Against moles and mice (Mole plant is a species of Euphorbia)

NASTURTIUM: Against aphids, squash bugs, striped pumpkin beetles, woolly aphids

PENNYROYAL: Against ants and plant lice

PEPPERMINT: Against white cabbage butterflies, ants

PETUNIA: Against beetles

POT MARIGOLD: Against asparagus beetles, tomato worms and many other insects

PYRETHURM: Against pickleworms, aphids, leafhoppers, spider mites, harlequin bugs, imported cabbage worms and ticks

ROSE GERANIUM: Oil or crushed leaves as insect repellants

ROSEMARY: Against cabbage moths, bean beetles, carrot flies, malaria mosquitoes

RUE: Against Japanese beetles

SAGE: Against cabbage moths, carrot flies, ticks

SANTOLINA: Against moths

SASSAFRAS: Against plant lice

SOUTHERNWOOD: Against cabbage moths, malaria mosquitoes

SPEARMINT: Against ants, aphids

STINGING NETTLE: Against aphids, black flies

SUMMER SAVORY: Against bean beetles

TANSY: Against flying insects, Japanese beetles, striped cucumber beetles, squash bugs and ants

THYME: Against cabbage worms

WHITE GERANIUM: Against Japanese beetles

WORMWOOD: Against animal intruders, cabbage worm butterflies, black flea beetles, malaria mosquitoes

Intercropping. This is really the heart of companion planting, for the idea is to have two or more different vegetables growing in the same piece of ground, or in the same row, providing diversification. And this idea need not be confined to vegetables only. Flowers and herbs can happily bump shoulders with each other. In fact, they *should*.

If your garden is small and you don't want to have empty spaces between your pea and bean rows, intercrop with broccoli, Brussels sprouts, cabbages, cauliflower, kale or even radishes or carrots. After the early peas and beans are out, the slower-growing vegetables have all the space to themselves, and you have room to walk again. This may make things a bit cramped at times, but if you have little space and a short growing season it's well worth trying. Of course to be successful you must keep up the fertility of your soil as well.

I like to keep a sort of "floating crop game" going in my own garden, making small plantings of quick-growing vegetables which sprout readily from seed: such as lettuce, radish, spinach, celery, cabbage, kale, chard, collards and other greens. Staggered plantings mean fresh supplies coming on all through the season.

Plants that will help each other are put together as often as possible, either in the same row, (as marigolds with bush beans), or in adjacent rows. Lettuce and onions do well together so I pop in a lettuce plant each time I pull a green onion for the table. I plant onions close together, pull every other one, letting the remaining onions mature for dry onions. In my climate even eggplant and green peppers benefit from a bit of shade, so I plant these together in a row next to okra.

Many vegetables are pretty enough to put in the flower beds. Parsley between bulbs, provides an attractive background in the spring. Tomatoes can grow with roses and at the same time protect them against black spot. Many vine crops such as squash, cucumbers and pumpkins grow well with corn and may even protect it from raccoons. The corn is helpful in protecting vine crops from wilt. Many early crops do well following spinach, which is rich in saponin. Early spinach also may be intercropped between straw-berries.

Chive clumps are another attractive planting (see CHIVE for benefits) that grow larger each year in the rose garden, late spring bringing a pincushion of lavender blossoms that last for many days.

Hardy amaryllis, a member of the lily family, sends out long strap leaves in early spring. After the leaves ripen and die the ground is bare until August when a sturdy stem emerges to grow quickly and bear fragrant pink lilies. A lettuce planting between the bulbs contrasts with the flower making it far more beautiful.

Some vegetables have been especially hybridized for ornamen-tation in a flower planting. Flowering cabbage and kale come in colorful shades of red, white and green yet have excellent flavor. Plant them with the same mints and thyme, rosemary, sage, hyssop, as the garden varieties.

In garden intercropping, try not to put a plant that needs light where other, taller growing plants will shade it, nor a moisture-loving plant with another that is greedy for water.

Just follow the general rules: asparagus with tomatoes, beans with carrots or summer savory, beets with onion or kohlrabi, mem-bers of the cabbage family with aromatic plants or potatoes or celery, leeks with onions, celery or carrots, or turnips with peas.

Remember also the dislikes, and do not plant beans with onion, garlic or gladiolus, beets with pole beans, the cabbage family with strawberries, tomatoes or pole beans, or potatoes with pump-kin, squash, cucumber, sunflower, tomato or raspberry.

J

Jerusalem Artichoke (*Helianthus tuberosus*).   In Italy these are called "girasole," meaning "turn with the sun" and they really are a type of sunflower and should not be confused with the globe artichoke, which is an entirely different plant.

Jerusalem artichokes, a native American plant, were known to and used by the Indians. They are a good companion to corn. The root is the edible portion, for this sunflower has its surprise at the bottom, the flowers being attractive but not large.

The principle food content of the Jerusalem artichoke is inulin, a tasteless, white, polysaccharide dissolved in the sap of the roots, and which can be converted into levulose sugar. This is of special interest to diabetics, for levulose is highly nutritious and the sweetest of all known natural sugars. Levulose also occurs in most fruits in the company of dextrose, but in the Jerusalem artichoke it is present alone. The artichokes are high in food value and rich in vitamins. They may be cooked or eaten raw in salads.

Jewelweed (*Impatiens biflora* or *I. pallida*). Jewelweed is an excellent remedy for poison ivy, relieving the itching almost instantly. It does not have an adverse effect on the poison ivy plants, for the two often grow side by side. In fact, wherever poison ivy grows, jewelweed is likely in the vicinity.

To make the remedy, boil a potful of jewelweed until the liquid is about half the original volume. The strained juice is effective

Jewelweed often grows with poison ivy, blooms between July and September, is a remedy for the itch of the poison ivy and for stinging nettle.

Poison ivy is a dangerous skin irritant to most people. Its woody vine climbs by means of aerial rootlets on the stems. (See page 129.)

both in preventing the rash after exposure and in treating the rash after it has developed. The best way to keep the extract is frozen and stored in cubes in the freezer. Pack them in small plastic bags and they will be at hand if needed.

The young, tender sprouts of jewelweed are edible also, cooked like green beans.

K

Kale (*Brassica oleracea acephala*). This cool weather crop is fine to grow in the fall garden, and it will stand most average winters if given a little protection.

Kale does well in the same rows as late cabbage or potatoes. If planted about the first of August, following late beans or peas, it will continue to grow until a hard freeze. A light freeze does not hurt it and even improves its flavor.

Wild mustard and kale sometimes are a problem in oat fields. Rolling is the best method of control. It should be practiced early in the morning while the plants are still wet with dew. The springy oats will pop back up again but the mustard or kale will be broken.

Kirlian Photography. This is a method of photographing plant, animal and human auras, first discovered by the Russians Semyon Davidovich Kirlian and his wife, Valentina.

One of their experiments using leaves from a healthy plant and from a diseased plant, showed an excellent picture of energy flares from the healthy one but only a weak facsimile from the other. The leaves, apparently identical to the human eye, were shown by the camera to be plainly different, illness evident in the plant's energy field being shown before becoming apparent as a symptom in its physical body.

Only the briefest evaluation of the Kirlian plant photography is possible here, but it is a fascinating possibility that sometime it will aid in unraveling the mystery of plant companionship.

Leaves placed between film and the electrodes of the Kirlian device show tiny flares of white, blue and even red and yellow surging out of what apparently are channels in the leaves. This effect is achieved only with healthy leaves, becoming distorted if the leaf is mutilated, and gradually diminishing as the leaf dies. The aura of a freshly-plucked leaf, according to Dr. Thelma Moss of the University of California, is a brilliant and colorful rosy pink, the colors gradually dimming and disappearing as the leaf dries up.

Knotweed (*Polygonum aviculare*). These members of the buckwheat family grow mostly on acid soils. The prostrate knotweed, frequently found on garden borders and along paths, doesn't mind being trampled on. All knotweeds are characterized by "knots" on their stems from which branches grow.

Knotweeds in pastures are thought to be troublesome to sheep. They also inhibit the growth of turnips, and are very rich in silica.

Kohlrabi (*Brassicaceae*). Kohlrabi grown with onions or beets, with aromatic plants, and surprisingly with cucumbers, are mutually beneficial in part because they occupy different soil strata. It dislikes strawberries, tomatoes and pole beans but helps protect the garden members of the mustard family.

It is a demanding plant, needing plenty of water but good drainage, as well as good supplies of compost. It grows best in filtered sunlight.

Korean Grass (*Zoysia japonica*). This group of eastern Asiatic, perennial creeping grasses, is widely used in the Southwest. Some are important horticulturally as lawn grasses, others as ornamentals. In hot, dry, climates Korean grass is strikingly effective planted with such succulents as the procelain-like aeonium, the texture contrast enhancing both plants. It grows well with *Cotyledon undulata* and the delicately beautiful rosettes of *Graptopetalum paraguayense*.

L

Ladybird Beetles.   These small black cousins of ladybugs have been found successful against fruit tree mites. In either the larval or adult stage they will consume an average of 11 mites an hour, according to the Pennsylvania State Research Laboratory at Biglerville.

Ladybugs.   These famous eaters of aphids may be purchased for garden release. The problem, especially in small gardens, is to keep them there. If there is a real need for their services and there is plenty of ladybug food around they are more likely to stay.

The way you release them will make a difference. Do not strew them about like grains of corn but rather place them by handfuls—carefully—around the base of infested plants. Their natural instinct is to climb the nearest plant and start hunting for food. Do your "seeding" gently, since rough handling, especially in warm weather, may excite them to flight. Early morning or evening is the best time.

Lamb's quarters, which sometimes harbor the leaf miner, also may play host to the beneficial ladybug. Newly-placed ladybugs are dependent on their hosts (which also may be Chinese celery, cabbage or other plants), and they must find aphids in sufficient quantity to keep them in the vicinity and assure reproduction. A female after one mating will produce from two hundred to one thousand offspring.

In the spring you can often find the eggs of ladybugs on the underside of leaves, near their early food supply, aphids. You will see them standing on end in clusters of 5 to 50, generally yellow or orange in color. The alligator-shaped larvae are blue-black and orange-spotted. (See SUPPLIERS INDEX.)

Lamb's Quarter (*Chenopodium album*).   This plant, sometimes called smooth pigweed, is one of our most enduring annual weeds, producing a tremendous amount of seeds that are able to survive dormant in the soil for decades. It is among the weeds that follow human footsteps and cultivation, liking a soil with a well-fermented humus.

Lamb's quarters are particularly stimulated when grown with potatoes, and they should be allowed to grow in the garden in moderate amounts, especially with corn. They also aid cucumber, muskmelon, pumpkin and watermelon as well as giving additional vigor to zinnias, marigolds, peonies and pansies.

This plant, a close relative of spinach, also is good to eat. The young shoots may be cooked and eaten like asparagus. It is richer in vitamin C than spinach, far richer in vitamin A and, though not quite so rich in iron and potassium, is still a good source of these minerals. It is exceptionally rich in calcium.

Lamb's quarters is a freebie that everyone should know about, for it is found in cultivated ground from North to South and East to West, and plants in the right stage for eating can usually be found from late spring until frost. It even grows in the Andes at a height of 12,000 feet, and here has become an important substitute for rye and barley, which cannot survive at such an altitude.

Larkspur (*Delphinium consolida*).   Common larkspur's alkaloids —delcosine and delsoline—have been found effective against aphids and thrips. Wild larkspur is detrimental to cattle and too much may cause poisoning. Barley as a crop however, is a weed deterrent and will prevent wild larkspur or poppy from establishing themselves. It is thought to promote vigor in winter wheat.

Lavender (*Lavendula officinalis*).   Lavender in a 2 percent emulsion spray for cotton pests, kills somewhere between 50 to 80 percent within a period of 24 hours.

Few ticks are found in lavender plantations although neighboring woods and shrubs may harbor many. It has been used effectively as a mouse repellant, and lavender sachets are often put in woolen clothing to repel moths, while leaves scattered under woolen carpets are helpful for the same purpose.

The plant grows from seed very slowly. Both are obtainable from Nichols Garden Nursery. (See SUPPLIERS INDEX.)

Leaves. Leaves are the lungs of plants. During the growing season respiration goes on vigorously, the leaves also throwing off an imperceptible yet vast amount of water vapor. This is called transpiration in plants, and in animals perspiration. A white oak of average size throws off about 150 gallons of water in one summer day. In the absence of leaves, the bark of trees still carries on the work of respiration, for it is porous even where it is thickest. Notice the little raised dots on the smooth surface of twigs. These are lenticels or breathing pores, not holes likely to become clogged with dust but porous, corky tissue serving to filter the air as it comes in.

Leek (*Allium porrum*). Leek is one of the "heavy feeders" and should be planted in soil well-fertilized with rotted manure. Leeks are usually sold in the grocery store (at least where I live) with the roots still attached. I once bought several bunches and planted them; they grew well and propagated, and I've had leeks ever since.

Leeks are good plants to grow with celery and onions, and also are benefited by carrots. Returning the favor, leeks repel carrot flies.

Legumes. Farmers and gardeners learned a long time ago to rotate their crops to take advantage of the increased soil fertility produced by legumes. These are the plants like beans, peas, clover, peanuts and alfalfa on whose roots live nitrogen-fixing bacteria, which are able to combine nitrogen with sugars to form proteins. In the legumes these bacteria live on the roots in small swellings called nodules.

Clover, or some other legume, may be plowed under before planting a crop of wheat or corn the following season. The decaying legumes, rich in fixed nitrogen, increase the nitrogen content of the soil without the need for commercial fertilizers.

The steps in the nitrogen cycle can be traced in the growth and use of clover:

(1) Atmospheric nitrogen is changed into proteins by the action of nitrogen-fixing bacteria growing in nodules on the clover roots.

(2) After plowing under, the clover proteins become changed into ammonia by ammonifying bacteria.

(3) Ammonia is then changed into nitrates by nitrifying bacteria.

(4) Both ammonia and nitrates are used by other plants to form plant proteins.

All our garden plants are aided by association with peas and beans, and crop rotation in the garden that takes advantage of this is just as important as crop rotation anywhere else. Another plant to use as a second crop, after an earlier one is out, is peanuts, provided you have a long growing season.

On larger acreages lespedeza, kudzu and esparsette may be used to aerate the soil and put nitrogen into it, while winter vetch and soybeans make excellent cover crops. Legumes sown with a small amount of mustard are helpful to grapevines and fruit trees. Peanuts are excellent to grow in an orchard of newly set nut trees.

Lemon Balm (*Melissa officinalis*).   Lemon balm, often called the "bee herb," has long been famous for its delightful, lemon-scented foliage and honeyed sweetness. *Melissa,* the generic name, is Greek for honeybee, and there is a very old belief that bees will not leave the hive area if melissa grows near it. Pliny wrote, "when bees have strayed away they do find their way back home by it."

Melissa tea calms the nervous system and stimulates the heart, it is very relaxing and may even dispel headache or migraine. In pastures it increases the flow of cows' milk, and it is very good to give cows after calving in a tea with marjoram.

Lettuce (*Lactuca sativa*).   In spring I keep a supply of small lettuce plants growing in cold frames. When I pull every other green onion for table use I pop in lettuce plants. They will aid the onions, and the compost in the onion row will still be in good supply for the lettuce to feed on, while the onion will repel any rabbits.

Lettuce grows well with strawberries, cucumbers, carrots and it has long been considered good to team with carrots and radishes. Radishes grown with lettuce in summer are particularly succulent.

row with radishes
lettuce in rows 12" apart
salad bowl to slow bolting

Lettuce needs cool weather and ample moisture to make its best growth, and I find that the seed will not germinate in very hot weather. Already-started lettuce should have some summer shade.

Lily-of-the-Valley (*Convallaria majalis*). This delightfully fragrant garden flower, in Germany called the "Mayflower," grows wild in the southern Allegheny regions. It likes a rich, humusy soil and partial shade. Do not put narcissus with it in a vase as it will cause the narcissus to wither, perhaps because the leaves and flowers of lily-of-the-valley are poisonous. (See chapter on POISONOUS PLANTS.)

Loco Weed (*Astragalus mollissimus* and *A. diphysus*). Loco weed, a member of the Delphinium family, gets its name from the Spanish word for crazy, due to the strange actions of animals poisoned by it but of about a hundred different kinds, many that belong to the bean family, Leguminosae, are not known to be poisonous.

Strangely enough the poisonous effect of loco weed depends on the soil in which the plants grow, resulting from their ability to absorb poisonous elements from the soil. Both the green and the dry plants are poisonous, the symptoms varying somewhat in horses, cattle and sheep.

Horses become dull, drag their legs, seldom eat, lose muscle control, become thin and then die. Cattle react similarly, but sometimes they run about wildly, or stagger and bump into objects in their path. Sheep are less apt to be injured by the poison.

Ranchers destroy loco weed by cutting the roots about two inches below the surface. In the Eighties, the state of Colorado spent $200,000 attempting to eradicate this weed.

Locust (*Robina*). Sweet pea-type blossoms on a tree or pods like the pea's swinging from the twigs mean it's a member of the pod-bearing *leguminosea*, to which herbaceous and woody plants both belong.

The black locusts (*R. Pseudacacia, L.*) have nectar-laden, white flowers of "butterfly form," which honeybees (leading a host of

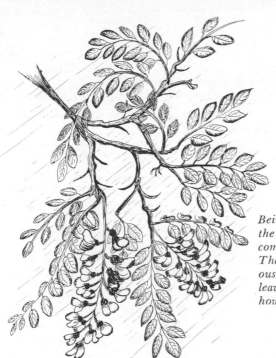

Being a leguminous tree the black locust is a good companion to lima beans. There are toxins dangerous to humans in the leaves, bark and roots, however.

other insects) swarm about as long as a flower remains to offer its sweet nectar. Cross-fertilization is the advantage the tree gains from all it gives.

Locust, good to plant as a border, has leaves, roots and bark that are poisonous if eaten, but the pods of honey locust (*Gleditsia triacanthos, L.*) contain a sweetish pulp used as cattle feed and occasionally by small boys, who brave the tree's thorns to get them.

Lovage (*Levisticum officinale*). Lovage planted here and there will improve the health and flavor of other plants. It is one of the herbs that may be used to reduce the amount of salt used for seasoning and is delicious sprinkled on salads or used in cheese biscuits. In dishes that need strengthening, it can replace meat stock, is excellent in soups and casseroles.

Lovage will winter well, but in colder climates the roots should have some protection.

Lupine (*Lupinus perennis*).   Sometimes called old maid's bonnets, wild pea or sun dial, the plant has vivid blue flowers, sometimes pink or white, with a butterfly shape that indicates its membership in the legume family.

Farmers once thought lupines preyed upon the fertility of their soil, hence the name derived from *lupus,* a wolf, while in fact they help corn to grow, as well as most other cultivated crops.

Lupines grow best on steep, gravelly banks or exposed sunny hills, liking almost worthless land where their roots can penetrate to surprising depths, in time leaving behind them fine, friable soil. They are adventurous pioneers, spreading far and wide in thrifty colonies, and are among the first plants to grow on the barren pumice after a volcanic eruption.

The lupine is one of those interesting flowers which go to sleep at night. Some fold their leaflets not only at night but also during the day when there is movement in the leaves. Sun dial, a popular name for the wild lupine, refers to this peculiarity. Among the nearly hundred kinds of lupines that grow in North America, some contain poisonous alkaloids, while the seeds of others can be eaten.

M

Maple (*Acer*).   The single genus *acer* includes from sixty to seventy species widely distributed over North America. *Acer saccharum,* the sugar maple, is the best known and economically the most important for both its beautiful wood and its sap which yields maple syrup. The black maple (*A. nigrum*) is the sugar maple of South Dakota and Iowa. Red maple (*A. rubrum, L.*), perhaps the most beautiful of all, is a swamp lover but will thrive on hillsides if the soil is moist, is widely planted in parks and along streets.

Maples have shallow, spreading root systems and it is difficult to get other plants to grow near them, perhaps because they may also excrete substances which inhibit the growth of some plants, particularly wheat. The maple leaves laid in layers between apples, carrots, potatoes and other root vegetables have a preservative effect.

Marigold (*Tagetes*).   These strong-scented beauties are very beneficial in discouraging nematodes which attack potatoes, strawberries, roses and various bulbs, especially if they are grown for several seasons in ground where nematodes are suspected. Experiments by P. M. Miller and J. F. Ahrens at the Experiment Station in New Haven, Conn. have shown that marigolds suppress meadow nematodes for up to three years, and control one or more other nematodes for one or more years without injuring the plants.

An easy way to use marigolds for nematode control is to rotate plantings of marigolds with crops that are susceptible to nematode injury. To lessen competition it is also wise to interplant marigolds two or more weeks after the plants which they are grown to protect.

Marigolds control nematodes by producing a chemical in the roots which kills them when it is released in soil. It is produced slowly so the marigolds must be grown all season to give lasting control. Interplanting them may not greatly help garden plants during the first season, but the benefits become apparent the following years, since the nematode population is reduced.

Tomatoes interplanted with marigolds will grow and produce better. Plantings with beans help protect against the Mexican bean beetle, while they help deter weeds and may be planted as a crop against invasions of ground elder, bindweed and ground ivy. The older types with strong odor in both foliage and blossom are considered the most useful.

Pot marigold (*Calendula officinalis*) or calendula planted in the vicinity of choice evergreens will repel dogs. This is an old-fashioned herb whose dried flowers were used by our grandmothers to flavor soups.   *yellow, gold, & orange - Tagetes varieties*

Marjoram (*Marjorana hortensis*).   This small, easily grown plant is probably one of the oldest herbs in use. "Marjoram" really cov-

boarder

ers three very different kinds of marjoram, all of which belong to the Labiatae family.

The sweet marjoram, an annual, is the most popular for flavoring, especially in sausages. It was used extensively by the Greeks who gave it the name, which means "joy of the mountains." Its disinfectant and preserving qualities made it an invaluable culinary herb in the Middle Ages.

Pot marjoram (see also under MARIGOLD), is a perennial with a bit less flavor but more easily grown.

Wild marjoram (*Oregano vulgare*) is a wild as well as cultivated variety with a strong flavor, the pungency varying according to where it grows. This herb, also known as oregano, is used the world over in Italian, Mexican and Spanish dishes, and is believed to have both stimulating and medicinal properties, since it contains *thymol*, a powerful antiseptic when used internally or externally. The whole plant of oregano is covered with hairy oil glands. The pleasant aromatic scent, reminiscent of thyme, is very lasting —even the dead leaves and stems retain it during the winter or when dried for culinary use.

In the garden all the marjorams have a beneficial effect on nearby plants, improving both growth and flavor.

Mayweed (*Anthemis cotula*).   Sometimes this is called dog fennel or fetid camomile because of its evil smell. Beekeepers used to rub it into their skin to repel bees, and it also will repel fleas and may be rubbed into floors and walls of a granary to repel mice.

Meadow Pink (*Lychnis floscuculi*).   The roots of all members of the lychnis family contain saponin which produces a soapy foam if stirred in water. Before the invention of soap these roots, together with the true saponaria, were used for washing. An interesting family member is the sleepy catchfly, so called because its flowers are closed most of the day, opening only in bright sunshine, while the gluey substance on its stems entangles flies.

Meadow Saffron (*Colchicum autumnale*).   This plant blooms in fall, and will do so even without soil around its poisonous bulbs.

Colchicum, the source of a present-day drug derived from the bulbs, is used to treat gout and also has been used to produce doubling of chromosomes in plants.

Melon (*Cucurbitaceae*).   Crop rotation can be one of your best weapons against garden pests, but do not rotate melon, squash or cucumber with each other, since all are cucurbits.

Timing is another weapon. Most cucurbits are not very susceptible to borers once they are past the seedling stage, so try either earlier or later plantings. I find fall-planted cucumbers and squash are almost entirely insect-free.

Do not plant melons near potatoes, though they will grow well with corn and sunflowers. Morning glory is thought to stimulate the germination of melon seeds.

Heavy waxed paper placed under melons helps to keep worms from entering, while sabadilla dust is effective, too. Melon leaves, rich in calcium, are good to place on the compost pile.

Mice.   Mice and rats are repelled by fresh or dried leaves or the oils of mints, by camphor and pitch pine. Mothballs repel rabbits as well as mice but should not be used where food crops are grown.

If mice like your garden too well, repel them with bulb plantings of daffodils, narcissi, scilla or grape hyacinths.

Sea onions, white lavender, wormwood and corn camomile (*A. arvensis*), and spurge repel mice, while everlasting pea is useful against field mice and leaves of dwarf elder against mice in granaries.

Mildew, Powdery (*Erysiphacea*).   Mildew is a fungus of the type called an "obligate parasite" because it feeds on living plants. When moisture conditions are just right, wind-carried spores (little seeds) resting on a plant's leaves send out germ tubes which grow into white threads (mycelia), which branch over them in a white, soft, felty coating. This type of fungus does not grow *inside* the plant but sends its little suckers (haustoria) into the plant's sap. As chains are built up from the mycelium spores the plant becomes covered in a few days. Eventually black fruiting bodies with the sexual or "overwintering" spores are formed.

Because it is on the surface, mildew is more easily controlled than many other fungi, and horsetail tea is an excellent spray to use. During the season when green plants are available it is good to prepare an extract by covering freshly-picked plants with water. Allow them to ferment for about 10 days, then dilute the liquid and use it as a spray in the same way as the tea. Mustard seed flour or sulphur dust also may be used, while polybutenes, oil derivatives, have been used successfully to control powdery mildew on cucurbits.

Milk.   Cows and goats give more and richer milk when fed on stinging nettle hay or members of the Umbelliferae family. We always saved discarded carrots and carrot tops when we kept milk goats, which also liked prunings from rose bushes if the thorns were not too prominent.

Skim milk may be used as a spray on tobacco and other plants subject to mosaic virus, and on peppers and tomatoes grown in the greenhouse. Pickers in commercial pepper and tomato plots find it useful to dip their hands in skim milk to avoid transmitting the mosaic virus, while whey proteins are effective, too.

A milk and blood spray has been used in orchards to control fungi and a milk and coal tar mixture against chinch bugs.

Sour milk or buttermilk may be sprinkled over cabbages against cabbage worms while milk mixed with white hellebore will kill flies, mice and rats. (See also Cows.)

Milkweed (*Asclepias*).   All of the many milkweeds exude milky juice when their leaves or stems are punctured. Roots are considered poisonous, but the Indians use them for various maladies, and some say that the juice cures warts or ringworm. Cows dislike the bitter, acrid plants but may eat them if hard pressed for food.

Milky Spore Disease (*Bacillus popilliae*).   This widely-used bacterial organism gives protection against the Japanese beetle by producing a fatal disease in the grub. Because it brings about an abnormal white coloring in the insect, it was called "milky."

It was developed in 1933 when a field survey in central New Jersey discovered a few abnormally white Japanese beetle grubs, which examination showed were teeming with bacterial spores.

This disease was studied by the Bureau of Entomology & Plant Quarantine where attempts were made to culture it for release. Treatment with the milky spore on experimental plots showed a more than 90 percent mortality in two months. In areas where the disease had been established naturally, equally high kills were found. This disease, occurring naturally in Japan, has kept the beetle from becoming a serious problem there.

The spore ordinarily needs only one application and then continues and spreads itself. It can be applied to the soil at any time except on a windy day or when it is frozen, but it is best to treat mowed or cropped areas. Apply a teaspoonful of the spore disease powder on grass or sod spots three to four feet apart and in rows the same distance apart. The beetle grub feeding in the soil will then take in the bacteria spores.

When a healthy grub becomes infected the spores give rise to slender vegetative rods, which multiply in the blood by repeated divisions. In a short time the normally translucent blood of the grub will become milky in appearance and eventually the grub dies. The spores stored in the body cavity then are released in the soil and are taken up by other grubs which in turn become infected. As the cycle continues the spores increase in number and, since more grubs are killed, fewer and fewer adult beetles emerge to feed on crops. The disease is cumulative and self-perpetuating.

Less effective but still useful methods of combatting the Japanese beetle include companion planting geraniums among roses and grapes to drive the beetles away. Larkspur eaten by the beetles will kill them, while soybeans work as a trap crop. The beetles are rarely destructive to cabbage, carrots, cauliflower, eggplant, onions, lettuce, parsley, peas, potatoes, radishes, spinach, squash, sweet potatoes, tomatoes and turnips.

Milky spore disease is sold under several trade names. (See SUP-PLIERS INDEX.)

Minerals in Plants.   Many weeds seem to have a mysterious capacity for enriching soils. Jimson weeds (*datura*) grown near pumpkins will promote their health and vigor; the best watermelons come from the weediest part of the patch; onions grown with weeds (but not allowed to be overwhelmed) are apt to be larger than those in clean cultivated rows.

This is particularly true if the weeds are the so called "deep divers" which break up the subsoil, allowing the roots of the vegetable plants to have a larger-than-usual feeding zone. Deep divers sometimes bring up from below the hardpan mineral elements which the roots of food plants cannot reach. The high mineral content of weeds is another reason for adding them to the compost pile. (See COMPOST.)

Miniclimate.   A miniclimate is something you can take advantage of if you have an unusual natural feature on your land, such as a pond which tempers air temperatures. Or you can create a miniclimate yourself by varying your plantings, adding a hedge or covering a fence with vines. A hedge makes a permanent windbreak, but rows of tall corn will quickly and seasonally serve the same purpose to shade and protect and limit air circulation on tender plants. So will vine plantings, such as grapes, and also cucumbers, which must be kept well watered during the summer, particularly if they take the western sun.

If you are fortunate enough to have water on your land you may be able to grow a number of moisture-loving plants such as blueberries, which are not possible for your neighbor just a mile or two down the road.

Mint (*Mentha*). Mint is a good companion to cabbage and tomatoes, improving their health and flavor. Both mint and tomatoes are strengthened in the vicinity of stinging nettle. Mints such as apple, orange or pineapple will thrive under English walnut trees, in part because of the filtered sunlight.

Mint deters the white cabbage worm by repelling the worm's butterflies. Spearmint may help to keep aphids off nearby plants, because the ants (which place the aphids on the plants) do not like mint. (See also PEPPERMINT and SPEARMINT.)

Mint is a repellant against clothes moths when used indoors, and is useful against black flea beetles. The leaves strewn under rabbit cages will keep flies to a minimum, while dried leaves (or mint oils) will repel rats and mice.

Spearmint repels ants, and for that reason controls aphids while possibly repelling rodents, too.

Mistletoe (*Loranthaceae*).   This parasite, is the most legendary of plants. It was sacred to the ancient Druids who cut it with a golden sickle (the symbol of the sun), and caught it in a cloth to prevent it from touching the ground. Mistletoe also grows on apple trees, oak and poplar, usually being sown by birds. Here in Oklahoma it is our state "flower" and it grows profusely on hackberry trees.

People used to call the mistletoe "all heal," and thought there was no illness it could not cure. It is in fact poisonous, particularly the berries. If you find it growing on your trees remove it for it is a parasite and eventually will weaken the tree and possibly kill it.

Molasses Grass (*Mellimus minutiflora*).   This is one of Nature's very own insect traps. The covering of glandular hairs exudes a viscous oil capable of trapping small insects such as ticks. It does not kill them, but stops them from crawling upward to come in contact with an animal. Cattle pastured on this grass in Guatemala were found to be free of ticks within a year, and it has been planted in Florida with good results, at the same time it provides good forage for cattle which like to graze on it. It also repels mosquitoes and the tsetse fly.

Mole (*Gryllidae*).   Moles generally are considered a nuisance and they do consume beneficial creatures such as earthworms, but they also feed on Japanese beetles. They are deterred by a few plants of caper spurge (*Euphorbia lathyrus*) strategically placed, by daffodil bulbs and castor bean plants. Thorny twigs of raspberry, rose, hawthorne or mesquite pushed into burrows will scratch the moles and cause them to bleed to death.

Morning Glory (*Ipomoea*).   The Indians liked to grow wild morning-glory with corn—probably one of the earliest examples of companion planting—since they believed it gave the corn added vigor. It is believed that morning-glory seeds also will stimulate the germination of many types of melon seed.

Kentucky Wonder beans and morning-glory planted on the same

Though parts of it are poisonous, the thorn apple is beneficial to pumpkins. (See Datura, page 49.)

The wild morning glory is good for corn, and in an orchard, too. (See also page 181.)

trellis will grow and blend together. I find that both will last all summer if kept well-watered.

Morning-glory seeds will germinate sooner if boiling water is poured over them before covering with soil. This does not harm the seeds and will soften the shell, causing the seeds to sprout more quickly. Other extra-hard coated seeds may be treated the same way.

This vine takes plant parenthood seriously and will vigorously re-seed itself.

Mosquitoes. Garlic-based oil (see GARLIC), is effective in killing mosquito larva in ponds, as will derris root or tuba, long so used by the Chinese. *Myristicin,* a synthesized compound found in parsnips, also is effective as a selective insecticide against the larva as is bacillus thuringiensis.

The leaves of molasses grass (*Mellimus minutiflora*) and sassafras are mosquito repellants, and I find that castor beans planted around my garden make it more pleasant to work there in the long, cool western twilights when I do most of my garden work.

Euell Gibbons says that American pennyroyal (*Hedeoma pulegioides*), sometimes called squaw mint and a native American plant not to be confused with the European pennyroyal (*Mentha pulegium*), is a natural insect repellant. A handful crushed and rubbed on the skin will not only emit a pleasant smell but also repel mosquitoes and gnats. (See SHEPHERD'S PURSE.)

Moths and Millers.   If moths and millers are troublesome in fruit trees, place one cup molasses in 1 1/2 cups water and hang in small buckets or cans from the limbs. Remove the insects occasionally or make new solutions. This remedy is particularly helpful if used in peach trees.

Mugwort (*A. vulgaris lactiflora*).   Mugwort is one of the most useful members of the Artemisias family. Planted in chicken yards it will help repel lice, and since the chickens like it as a food it is also thought to be helpful in ridding them of worms. Made into a weak tea it may be used as a fruit tree spray, too.

Mugwort is not good too near other garden plants because it has a growth-retarding effect, particularly in years of heavy rainfall. The roots exude a toxic substance and also the leaves. This soluble toxic, absinthin, washed off by rain, soaks into the soil near the plant and remains active over an indefinite period of time.

Mulberry (*Morus alba, M. rubra, M. nigra*).   White mulberry is the chosen food of silkworms and no substitute has ever removed this tree's preeminence. The berries of the red mulberry (*M. rubra*) do not compare with the cultivated type, but are of value in poultry yards and hog pastures where they are eagerly devoured. The black mulberry (*M. nigra*), believed a native of Persia, has large, dark red, juicy fruits but is hardy only in the Southern and Pacific Coast states where it is a desirable tree because it is so attractive to birds.

Mulberry trees are particularly good for grapes to be trained to grow on. Tree-grown grapes are more difficult to pick, but they will be relatively free from fungus diseases due to better circulation of air around them. Worms in horses may be repelled by mulberry leaves, and Russian mulberry is sometimes used as a trap crop to protect cherries and strawberries.

Mulch. Mulch can be almost anything that retards loss of moisture, but organic mulches which add nutrients to the soil are considered the most helpful. These include chopped bark, buckwheat hulls, cocoa shells, coffee grounds, corncobs, cottonseed hulls, cranberry vines, evergreen boughs, grass clippings, hay, hops, leaves (particularly oak leaves which repel slugs, cutworms and grubs of June bugs), manure, peanut hulls, peat moss, pine needles (great to increase stem strength and flavor of strawberries), poultry litter, salt hay, sawdust, seaweed, stinging nettle, straw, sugar cane residue, tobacco stems and wood chips and shavings. Particularly comprehensive data is found in *The Mulch Book* by Stu Campbell. (See SUGGESTED READING.)

Mustard (*Brassica alba*). White mustard (*B. kaber*) and black mustard (*B. nigra*), are said to reduce the populations of certain nematodes, but many farmers regard them as a nuisance because they feel they deplete the soil.

The root secretions of mustard are considered helpful on an acid or over-mineralized soil in need of healing. Sow (not over 15 percent) mustard with anything from legumes to grapevines and fruit trees or use mustard as a cover crop for alfalfa.

Mustard also contains an oil attractive to several groups of insects, and so may be planted as a catch crop to draw insects from cabbage, cauliflower, radish, kohlrabi, Brussels sprouts, turnips and collards. Because it acts as a host plant to various insects and diseases it should be removed and destroyed before the main crops can be harmed.

Wild mustard in oat fields can be controlled by rolling early in the day while the plants are still wet with dew. The more flexible oats will spring back up, but the mustard plants will be broken.

Mycorrhizae. One of the most interesting and helpful relationships between fungi and higher plants is found in mycorrhizae. This, simply put, is a combination of a fungus with the root of some species of higher plant. Mycorrhizae occur in many species of herbs, shrubs and trees all over the world and most woody plants appear to have them.

Mushrooms form important mycorrhizal associations with evergreens and other plants and are able to convert rock materials into valuable agriculture soils.

The fungi of mycorrhizae belong to various classes, but mycorrihizal roots differ in certain structural features from uninfected roots, often being short and thick and commonly lacking root caps and root hairs. Sometimes they do not branch.

The physiological and biological significance of these fungi is not fully understood, but most scientists now believe that the relationship between them and the roots they inhabit is beneficial to both.

According to this view the fungi receive food from root tissues and in turn facilitate certain physiological activities of the roots. Some investigators believe the fungi increase water absorption of roots, others that the fungi promote the absorption of certain organic nitrogenous substances from the soil, or that they carry on nitrogen fixation much as is done by the nitrogen-fixing bacteria.

That the fungi may have beneficial effect is supported by many observations and experiments. For instance, if seedlings of certain pine trees are grown in sterile soils, or in soils without suitable species of mycorrhizal fungi, the growth of seedlings is weak and slow. But if the soil is inoculated with these fungi and they infect the roots, the seedling growth increases quickly and conspicuously, indicating a condition of mutual benefit.

N

Narcissus (*Amaryllidaceae*).   A planting of African marigolds (*Tagetes erecta*) a year before planting narcissus bulbs will defeat certain nematodes which often attack the bulbs. This is because of sulphur-containing substances called *thiophenes* present in the root exudates of the marigolds. The French marigolds (*Tagetes patula*) have similar root excretions.

Nasturtiums (*Tropaeolum*).   Nasturtiums planted with squash will keep away squash bugs, but be sure to give the flowers a head start since the squash grow more quickly. If aphids appear in the nasturtiums—a sign there is a lime deficiency in your soil—dust the plants with lime and they will disappear.

Bouncing bet, sometimes called soap-wart, is one of many plants that contain saponin, a lathering substance which also when decomposed helps to retain soil moisture. (See page 146.)

Nasturtium repels a wide range of harmful insects from vegetables and fruits, planted nearby or made into a spray. It also improves growth and flavor in the neighbor crops.

Nasturtiums sown in a greenhouse will help to repel white flies; in the garden when planted near broccoli will keep down aphids and benefit potatoes, radishes, cucurbits and any member of the cabbage family. Under apple trees they will protect against woolly aphis.

Sprays made from nasturtium leaves may be used on the same crops which benefit from the nasturtium plants. Add a small amount of soap powder so the sprays will cover and adhere better.

Nematodes.   These microscopic nuisances are discouraged by marigolds, scarlet sage (*Salvia*) or dahlias (*Dahlia*). Soils rich in organic matter discourage nematodes, while asparagus is a natural nematicide. Tomatoes grown near asparagus thus are protected, while in turn the tomatoes protect the asparagus from the asparagus beetle. (See EELWORMS.)

Nettles.   (See STINGING NETTLE.)

Nitrogen-Fixing Plants.   Though nitrogen makes up 80 percent of the volume of the atmosphere, it is almost useless to most plants, for it must be changed into a compound before it can be used. Lightning combines or fixes small amounts of this nitrogen and oxygen in the air, thus forming oxides of nitrogen which are washed out of the atmosphere by rain or snow to reach the soil.

Nitrogen-fixing bacteria living in nodules on the roots of legumes, however, can change atmospheric nitrogen into nitrogen compounds useful to themselves and other plants. These bacteria also change the atmospheric nitrogen into proteins in the roots of alfalfa, beans, clover, esparsette, kudzu, lespedeza, peas, peanuts, soybeans, winter (hairy) vetch, and other leguminous plants. Farmers for centuries have rotated their crops to take advantage of this increased soil fertility produced by legumes.

Legumes benefit not only themselves by the nitrogen-fixing bacteria but other plants nearby. Peas and beans, for instance, benefit potatoes, carrots, cucumbers, cauliflower, cabbage, summer savory, turnips, radishes, corn and most other herbs and vegetables.

Clover is particularly beneficial if used as a green manure crop and plowed under before planting a crop of wheat or corn the following season. A green manure crop of alfalfa will benefit a crop of cotton. Red clover may be used on soils too acid and too poorly aerated for alfalfa. The optimum pH for red clover is between 5.8 and 6.8 but it can stand a pH below 6.0 and still do reasonably well.

Nitrogen-Fixing Trees.   Black alder (*Ilex verticillata*) adds nitrogen to the soil. It is the only known nonleguminous shrub that has root nodules which can do this. It also helps to drain wet soil.

Pod-bearing trees have the power to take nitrogen out of the air and store it in their roots and stems. The decay of these parts restores to the soil the plant food that is most often lacking and most expensive to replace. These trees and shrubs include: Black locust (*Robinia pseudacacia*), bristly locust (*Robinia hispida*) (sometimes called rose-acacia), clammy locust (*Robinia viscosa*), scotch broom (*Robinia scopariua*), honey locust (*Gleditsia triacanthos*), Kentucky coffee tree (*Gymnocladus dioicus*), redbud (*Cercis canadensis*) (sometimes called Judas tree), yellow-wood (*Cladrastis lutea*), woad waxen (*Genista tinctoria*) (sometimes called dyer's greenwood), indigo bush (*Amorpha fruticosa*) (sometimes called false indigo), mesquite (*Prosopis juliflora*), screw-bean (*Prosopis pubescens*) (a slender-trunked mesquite, sometimes called screw-pod), Palo Verde acacia (*Cercidium Torreyanum*), Jamaica dogwood (*Icthyomethia Piscipula*), horse bean (*Parkinsonia aculeata*), Texas ebony (*Zigia flexicaulis*) and frijolito (*Sophora secundiflora*).

Nurse Grass.   A quick-germinating and quick-growing grass such as redtop frequently is used in lawn seed mixtures to provide a rapid ground cover which helps to crowd out weeds during the early development of the more permanent grasses such as Kentucky blue grass. The blue grass may take two or three years to reach full development, but once it attains this under favorable conditions, it will crowd out the nurse grass.

Nurse Trees.   As abandoned fields again become covered with vegetation, the brushland is gradually reforested. The first trees are quick-growing, short-lived types which provide conditions suitable for the slower-growing, longer lived trees. Looking at the forest floor, you will see very few pine seedlings. Other seedlings—young oaks, black cherries and hickories—do better. Gradually the pines will die off and the young hardwoods grow up and take their place. Should a forest fire occur, the whole process will start over again.

Nut Grass (*Chufa*).　The chufa is almost as old as civilization, the ancient Egyptians developing cultivated strains more than five thousand years ago. The botanical name, *Cyperus esculentus* means an "edible sedge," and the chufa is related to the tules and bulrushes. The "nut" of the chufa, which is really a tuber, may be made into many tasty and unusual dishes. But consider well before growing this plant, for it can become a fearful weed. Having battled against it in my garden for many years, I have come to the conclusion that this is a plant that only Euell Gibbons could love.

If the native species of chufa plagues you, it can be discouraged by growing a heavy cover crop of cowpeas on the plot for several summers. Sow the cowpeas so thickly as to form a thick mat to shade the soil. Plow them under in late fall, in October or November, and they will add nitrogen to the soil. St. Augustine grass will choke out chufa on a lawn.

Nut Trees.　Nut trees are good to plant in pastures and near stables, manure and compost piles, to repel flies on cattle. Walnut leaves placed where dogs or cats sleep will repel fleas. (See chapter on POLLINATION.)

O

Oak (*Quercus*).　Oaks grown with American chestnuts seem to give them some resistance to chestnut blight. During growth oaks accumulate a large amount of calcium in their bark, yet amazingly the most calcium has been found in the ash of oak trees that grew in calcium-deficient soil.

A mulch of oak leaves serves to control radish and turnip maggots as well as repelling slugs, cutworms and grubs of June bugs, but some gardeners believe the leaves have an inhibiting effect on certain vegetables, thus should be fully composted before being spread on the garden.

In Germany it has long been a practice to control greenhouse pests such as ants, aphids and small mites with the smoke from oak leaves. The smoke is not considered poisonous, will not kill bacteria in the soil nor leave harmful residues.

Live oaks are believed to exert a protective influence on citrus trees.

The trichogramma wasp, whose larvae feed on moth eggs, helps keep oak trees green by controlling gypsy moths. Bacillus thuringiensis will also control and kill various caterpillars on the trees.

Oat (*Avena sativa*).   There are some seeming contradictions in companion planting. One gardener reports that her unthrifty young peach trees apparently were assisted by moldy oats from the cleanings of the oat bin when applied one bushel to each tree. After several weeks all her slow-growing trees were putting out new, healthy leaves. On the other hand another gardener feels that root excretions from oats inhibit the growth of apricot trees.

A possible reason for the good growth of the peach trees is the mold, rather than the oats, for almost all trees have a symbiotic relationship with some fungi (including molds). The fungi grow around the plant roots and furnish vitamins and other natural compounds necessary for a fast-growing and healthy tree.

This brings us back to the soil again. Because of this relationship it's a good idea to have some of the original soil packed around the roots when transplanting a shrub or tree. Quite likely there will be fungi in the soil beneficial to the plant.

You may even do this: If you have a tree that isn't doing well after being set the first time, take some soil from another tree of the same variety which *is* growing well and dig it in around your problem tree. There's a good chance that your tree will perk up and grow.

This will work well not only with trees but with other ornamentals and even with house plants. If possible investigate the original, invigorating habitat of such plants, remove some of the soil and see if Nature doesn't have a cure for the ailing plant far better than any commercial fertilizer you could buy.

Certain planting sequences are desirable: A cover crop of mixed clover and oats following sod and before corn is planted, will lessen the white grubs that infest corn. Oats and vetch do well planted together.

Oats sometimes can be grown effectively as a trap crop to lure redwing blackbirds away from other grain crops. The stand should be grown at some distance from the birds' roosting places. See "Insect-Resistance in Crop Plants" in SUGGESTED READING for data in oats with "built-in" insect resistance.

Oil from Plants.   According to Dr. Donald L. Klass of the Institute of Gas Technology in Chicago, it may be possible to produce synthetic natural gas in commercial quantities from plants. It already has been done in the laboratory by a process very similar to that used to convert coal into gas.

Plants, however, are much less expensive to produce than coal, and the synthetic natural gas is reported to be just as good. Also it is possible to use any kind of plant available, even apparently useless weeds. Furthermore it is not necessary to use good, cultivated soil, so such plants as cactus, sagebrush and other types of plants which require little water can be grown for this use in desert areas. Even algae or water hyacinth could be planted in lakes now too polluted for other purposes.

If further research proves this project practical we might have a perpetual source of energy from plants that have captured it through photosynthesis from the sun.

Oil from plants is not a new idea, for it has long been extracted from such trees as the tung and olive. This is a little different from the "essential oils" found in herbs.

Tung oil, extracted from the three to five kernels inside the nut, is widely used in paints, varnishes, lacquers and printing inks. Oils from safflowers, sunflowers and many other vegetable sources are made into cooking oils of the highest quality, far better for our health than products made of animal fat because they are poly-unsaturated.

Okra (*Hibiscus esculentus*).   This native of the Old World tropics is grown for its immature pods which are called okra or gumbo. It's a warm-weather plant that will grow wherever melons or cucumbers thrive. I plant two rows, dig a trench between, and cover it with mulch. On the north side of my okra I plant a row of sweet bell peppers and on the south side a row of eggplant. All are well mulched as the season advances. When the weather becomes dry in midsummer I lay the hose in the trench and flood it so that all three companions grow well.

Onion (*Allium cepa*).   Onions and all members of the cabbage family get along well with each other. They also like beets, straw-

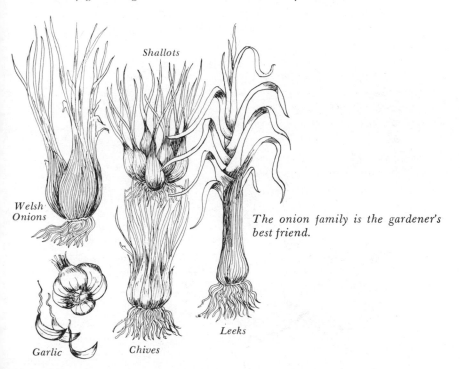

Shallots

Welsh
Onions

The onion family is the gardener's
best friend.

Garlic   Chives   Leeks

berries, tomatoes, lettuce, summer savory and camomile (sparsley), but do *not* like peas and beans.

Since onion maggots travel from plant to plant when set in a row, scatter your onion plants throughout the garden.

Toxic substances in the pigments of red and yellow onion skins appear to be associated with disease resistance. Russian biologist T. A. Tovstole found a water solution of onion skin, used as a spray three times daily at five-day intervals, gave an almost 100 percent kill of hemiptera, a parasite attacking more than a 100 different species of plants.

Opuntia (*Cactaceae*).   In the Southwest and Mexico people eat the flatleaved joints on opuntia cactus boiled or fried, and make the flowers into salads. The juicy fruits of opuntia are eaten raw or cooked, the seeds are ground up into a meal and made into cakes. The bushy cacti grow in hedges around houses, and where little else will survive they serve as windbreaks and ground cover.

The opuntia or prickly pear is often grown in hot areas as a hedgerow.

In some regions in times of drought ranchers 'burn off' the cactus spines so that cattle may eat the plants. Plant breeder Luther Burbank developed a spineless cactus that proved to be a useful source of food for both men and animals, and in some sections of California the opuntia type is a commercial crop. It is grown on sandy loam, fertilized with chicken manure and needs no insecticides. The crop of young leaves, which measure about eight inches long at one to two months, are hand-picked to be sold diced, shredded and spiced, or pickled.

Almost all of the many useful species of cactus will grow well with each other, requiring the same type of soil and cultural practices. Many have beautiful delicate blossoms and are grown as ornamentals, and there is a sub-zero cactus of the opuntia type which will grow in the North. (See SOURCES OF SUPPLY.)

Orach (*Atriplex hortensis*). This beautiful annual, sometimes called French spinach, has shield-shaped, wavy leaves of beet red. They have a mealy texture similar to its close relative, lamb's quarters, and are also used as a pot herb. While orach may be planted in the garden it should never be placed near potatoes, since it has an inhibiting effect on their growth.

Old-time herbalists believed that orach had a cleansing quality either raw or cooked and if laid upon swollen glands of the throat would cure the condition.

Oregano (*Origanum vulgare*). Sow with broccoli to repel the cabbage butterfly. (See MARJORAM.)

Origin of Plants. Some of our most valuable cultivated plants have never been found in the wild state, and others bear no resemblance to any known wild species.

This is interpreted as indicating a very ancient history of cultivation, since a cultivated species may have become so changed that it no longer resembles a wild ancestral species, or the wild ancestor may have died out. Thus the absence of wild ancestors of corn and of sugar cane is regarded as evidence of the great antiquity of their cultivation.

Botanists have reached some conclusions concerning the general geographical areas where important cultivated plants originated, and their relative ages of cultivation.

There is not a single species of important cultivated plant that is common to both the Old and the New Worlds. There also are many more plants of Old World origin than New.

Plants of Old World origin that have been cultivated for at least 4000 years (and probably longer) are: almond, apple, apricot, banana, barley, cabbage, date, eggplant, fig, flax, grape, hemp, mango, millet, olive, onion, peach, pear, rice, sorghum, soybean, watermelon and wheat.

Those cultivated for at least 2000 years, and possibly longer include: alfalfa, asparagus, beet, breadfruit, carrot, celery, cherry, chestnut, citrus fruits, cotton, lettuce, nutmeg, oats, pea, pepper (black), plum, poppy, radish, rye, sugar cane, tea, English walnut.

Plants cultivated for less than 2000 years are artichoke (globe), buckwheat, coffee, currant, gooseberry, muskmelon, okra, parsley, parsnip, raspberry, rhubarb and strawberry (some types).

Plants of New World origin (of unknown antiquity but certainly over 2000 and probably more than 4000 years) are: cacao (cocoa), corn, kidney bean, mate, sweet potato and tobacco.

Plants of more recent cultivation, some since the beginning of the Christian era, others before, are: avocado, cassava, cotton (some types), peanut, pineapple, potato, pumpkin, red peppers, rubber, squash, tomato and vanilla.

Osage Orange (*Maclura pomifera*).   This thorny tree is native from Arkansas to Texas and is hardy as far north as New England and central New York. It is valued for windbreaks, to grow in poor soils, and is an excellent hedge plant, being almost impenetrable when fully mature. It was widely planted by the pioneers as a living fence around their homes before barbed wire came into use. The name refers to the Osage Indians and to the yellow fruit which looks like an orange but is inedible.

Ox-eye Daisy (*Chrysanthemum leucanthemum*).   Ox-eye daisy seeds are beneficial in small quantity mixed (1 to 100) with wheat grains, but in larger quantity the daisy will overwhelm the wheat.

P

Pansy, Wild (*Viola tricolor*).   The wild form of the cultivated pansy is Shakespeare's "heartsease," and once was listed in the *U.S. Pharmacopoeia* as a medicine. Many species of viola were candied as a sweet and were thought to be soothing and therapeutic to the heart.

Rye helps the wild pansy to germinate and is itself seemingly improved by a few pansies. But the pansy has an inhibiting effect on wheat.

Parsley (*Petroselinum hortense*).   Parsley mixed with carrot seed helps to repel carrot flies by its masking aroma. It protects roses against rose beetles. Planted with tomatoes or with asparagus it will give added vigor to both.

Poultry are sometimes turned loose at intervals in parsley patches where there are many parsley worms, which are the larvae of the black swallowtail butterfly.

A number of different strains of parsley, including the *Hamburg*, (*Petroselinum crispum latifolium*), are grown solely for the fleshy roots which are cooked and eaten in the same way as parsnips.

Parsnip (*Pastinaca sativa*).   The parsnip is of ancient culture, but remains a vegetable for the special palate. The parsnips have few insect enemies and suffer from few diseases, but both the foliage and roots make a safe insect spray. They are not injured by freezing and are often left in the ground over winter. The seeds germinate slowly and unevenly and should not be used if over a year old.

Pea (*Pisum sativum*).   For large crops inoculate pea and bean seed with "Nitragen" (or similar compound), which is a natural bacterial agent. It coats the seed, aiding the plant by entering the sprouting seedling. This enables the plant more readily to form nodules on the roots which convert nitrogen from the air into a compound the plant can use.

Peas grow well with carrots, turnips, radishes, cucumbers, corn, beans and potatoes, as well as many aromatic herbs. They do *not* grow well with onions, garlic and gladiolus.

Always plow pea vines under or return them to the compost pile. Wood ashes used around the base of pea vines help to control aphids, while *myristicin,* a synthesized compound in parsnips, is a selective insecticide for pea aphids.

Peach (*Prunus persica*).　Never plant a young peach tree where an old one has been removed—plant a different fruit tree.

If peach leaf curl appears and only a few leaves are affected, pull them off by hand. Feeding the tree with well-rotted manure or compost high in nitrogen will help the tree back to health. Garlic planted close to the trunk will protect against borers. For more information on peach trees see chapter on **Pollination.**

Peanut (*Arachis hypogaea*).　As members of the legume family, peanuts are good soil builders. In many areas of the South and Southwest they may be grown as a second crop after an earlier one, such as carrots or beets, has been harvested. They make a good ground cover in an orchard of young nut trees.

Pear (*Pyrus*).　Some orchardists believe that pears are suppressed by the root excretions of grass, but a successful pear grower in California believing the opposite, lets a variety of grasses and weeds grow in his orchard.

This same grower sprays against codling moth and leaf roller using ryania because it is specific, killing only chewing insects. As a fertilizer he used chicken manure to provide nitrogen, plus cottonseed meal, compost, dried blood and other animal manures. (See chapter on **Pollination.**)

Pecan (*Hicoria pecan*).　Pecan trees like plenty of nitrogen. In the orchard plant a winter and spring cover crop such as clover, which harbors nitrogen-fixing bacteria. For a lawn specimen let a dense mat of grass grow near the trunk to conserve soil moisture and prevent sunscald of the roots. It is good to mulch with grass clippings, too.

The casebearer and hickory shuck worm, the most serious pecan pests, are best foiled by releasing trichogramma wasps in the orchard. Do not store pecan meats near onions or oranges.

Penny Cress (*Thlaspi arvens*).   Like shepherd's purse, this is often abundant where grain is grown. The seeds are 20 percent oil, and if accidentally ground with grain will spoil the flour. Mountain penny cress (*Thlaspi alpestre* var. *calaminare*) likes soils containing zinc.

Pennyroyal (*Mentha pulegium*).   Plant this with broccoli, Brussels sprouts and cabbage against cabbage maggot. Like tansy it may be grown at doorways to repel ants, and is also a good mosquito repellent if rubbed on the skin. Fresh or dried sprigs have long been used as a flea repellent.

Pepper, Herbs Used.   Basil, summer savory, thyme, marjoram and nasturtium can help replace pepper in cooking for those who have digestive disturbances.

Pepper, Hot (*Capsicum frutescens,* var. *fasciculatum* and var. *longum*).   Hot red peppers are among the most useful plants in the garden as well as the most flavorsome.

Use the slim cayenne peppers, grind and mix with water and a little powdered *real* soap to make an infusion to spray plants infested with aphids. Dry cayenne pepper may be dusted on tomato plants attacked by caterpillars.

However, if you note long green hornworms do not be too quick to spray. Watch to see if any of the tiny parasitic wasps which build noticeable white cocoons all over tomato hornworms are present. Do not harm these predators with sprays—they may be doing your work for you.

Ground red peppers placed around eggplants and rubbed on the leaves will help repel eggplant pests, and the dried pods, pulverized and sprinkled on corn silk, will give protection against raccoons.

Another all-purpose spray may be made of ground pepper pods, onions and a bulb of garlic. Cover this mash with water, let stand 24 hours and strain. Add enough water to make a gallon of spray. Use several times daily on roses, azaleas, chrysanthemums or beans to hold down serious infestations. Do not throw away the mash, but bury the residue among the plants where insects occur.

Peppermint (*Mentha piperita*). Of all herbs this makes the greatest demand on the soil for humus and moisture. It will benefit from a small amount of chicken manure if well broken down.

Peppermint drives away red ants from shrubs and planted among cabbage it will repel the white cabbage butterfly. When growing with chamomile it will have less oil but the chamomile will benefit and have more. The oil of peppermint is increased when it is grown with stinging nettle.

Black mint is distinguished from other species by purple stems and dark green leaves. It grows about three feet tall and is crowned with spikes of lavender flowers in midsummer. It is widely used for medicinal and commercial purposes. (See also MINT and SPEARMINT.)

Pepper, Sweet (*Capsicum frutescens*, var. *grossum*). The general requirements of sweet peppers are surprisingly like those of basil, so plant them together. Sweet peppers also grow well with okra, and since they are very brittle plants the okra, growing taller, serves as a windbreak. Bell Boy Hybrid

Peruvian Ground Cherry (*Nicandra physalodes*). When planted in quantity near a barn or in a stableyard it will repel flies, and it also is effective against white fly.

Petunia (*Petunia*). This is a member of the nightshade family, Solanaceae, the word derived from "petun," a South American name for tobacco since the tobacco plant belongs to the same family. Petunia protects beans against beetles.

pH. Experienced garden writers take for granted that everybody knows what pH is all about. But really it isn't scary at all. The pH of anything simply indicates its active acidity or alkalinity, expressed in units. It is generally used in horticultural science to indicate a condition of the soil, and it's important to know, because many plants thrive only when the pH value of the soil closely approximates the optimum for their particular kind.

Soil acidity may be of two kinds, active and potential. It is a state in which the concentration of hydrogen ion (H+) exceeds that of hydroxyl ions (OH−). When you have an exact balance of H+ and OH− ions, you have neutrality. When the OH− ions are greater than the H+ ions you have alkalinity.

Active soil acidity represents the excess of H ions over the OH ions present in the soil solution. It is expressed in pH units on the pH scale. On this scale 7 represents neutrality; higher readings indicate alkalinity, lower ones acidity. It is rare to find a soil with greater acidity than 3.5, or with greater alkalinity than 8.0. You should note, however, that the relationship between the figures is *geometric.* Acidity at pH 5 is ten times as great as at 6, and at pH 4, one hundred times.

Is there something you can do about it if a soil test shows too much one way or the other? Yes, to neutralize acidity the gardener adds lime, preferably the agricultural type. In my opinion all soil, but particularly alkaline ones, benefit from the use of compost or humus in the form of decomposed organic matter. A green manure crop plowed under also helps.

Pigweed (*Amaranthus retroflexus*). Pigweed pumps nutrients from the subsoil and loosens soil for such crops as carrot, radish and beet. It helps potatoes yield more abundantly and is good to grow with onions, corn, pepper and eggplant—but keep it thinned. Tomatoes grown with the weed are more resistant to insect attack.

Pine (*Pinus*). Pine boughs are good to lay over peonies in winter for protection. Remove in the spring before growth starts. Pine needles make a good mulch for azaleas, rhododendrons and other acid-loving plants and will increase vigor and flavor in straw-berries.

Pine needles contain terpene which, washed down by rain, has an inhibiting effect on seed germination. It is not good to place a compost heap near pine trees.

Plantain (*Plantago*).   Of the many different plantain species the large bracted plantain (*P. aristata*) is the most prolific, one plant producing well over 3000 seeds.

The narrow-leaved (*P. lanceolata*) has been used as a home rem-edy for treating bruises and strained joints. It also has a cooling and astringent effect if a few leaves are squeezed over a bee sting.

Plantain and red clover frequently are found growing together, this because the plantains occur as impurities in grass and clover seeds. If plantains appear on the lawn it is best to dig them out.

Plaintain benefits red clover but it is a weed that can get out of hand.

Poison Ivy (*Rhus radicans*).   Jewelweed will relieve the itching of poison ivy, (see JEWELWEED). If your homestead has poison ivy the best thing you can do is eradicate it. Mow close to the ground in midsummer and follow this with plowing and harrowing, grubbing out small patches. Under trees or along a fence where mowing might be difficult try smothering it with heavy cardboard or tar paper. A deep mulch of hay or straw may work as well.

Vines growing in trees may be cut near the ground and then pulled down a few days later. Be sure to wear gloves and protective clothing, washing well afterward, preferably with yellow soap. If there are many plants and burning seems advisable do not stand in the smoke, as the infection-causing oil may be carried to the skin.

Pokeweed (*Phytolacca americana*).   I find that pokeweed grows well under my figs, Scotch pines and other trees. Poke berries and roots are poisonous, but the tiny, pinkish-green, asparagus-like

Pokeweed is good with fig trees. Its roots and berries are poisonous but young shoots are safe and delicious when boiled.

shoots are simply delicious. Poke is one of the first greens to come up in early spring, and these shoots should be cooked lightly in several changes of water. The berries and roots contain *phytolaccin*, a cathartic and slightly narcotic substance used for treating rheumatism.

Poke should never be confused with the completely unrelated Indian poke, or white hellebore. This latter plant, also poisonous, grows in wet places and comes up very early in the spring before the edible poke starts growing.

Pollination.   (See chapter on POLLINATION.)

Poplar (*Salicaceae*).   The quick-growing, short-lived poplars often fulfill the function of "nurse trees." When a fire sweeps through the forest, it is likely to be the first tree to grow again on the bare land. The poplar's abundant seed much like willow's, is windsown far and wide. Lombardy poplars, which look like exclamation points, are often planted to shelter other plants from the wind.

Roland Clark of New Zealand writing in "The Nutshell" reports: "There seems to be a symbiosis between grass and poplars, and I expect to get more grass. I'll lose less moisture with a lower wind speed and I'll get a fair bonus each year from the prunings cut in midsummer—during our annual drought. The leaves are very palatable to stock." In Canada very good stock feed has been made by boiling poplar wood under pressure.

Poppy (*Papaver*).   Poppy and wild larkspur like to grow with winter wheat but dislike barley. Wheat fields heavily infested with poppy yield a poor harvest of lightweight seeds.

Poppies are grown for both seed and oil but they rob the soil of nutrients, causing it to need rest and reinforcement afterwards. This factor may be used to advantage, however, to choke out weeds which cannot be gotten rid of by any other means.

Poppy seeds may lie dormant in the ground for many years and then show up again with a grain crop, particularly winter wheat.

Poppies can become too much of a good thing, especially in plantings of barley, which it inhibits.

Potassium. Certain weeds indicate a soil rich in potassium: These are marsh mallow, knapweed, wormwood, opium poppy, fumitory, Russian thistle, tansy and sunflower. Red clover, however, is a good indicator of potassium deficiency. It will disappear with increasing acidity.

Tobacco takes up potassium in its leaves and stalks and is thus a good plant on the compost pile if it has not been sprayed with chemicals. Vegetables that like potassium are celeriac and leek.

Potato (*Solanum tuberosum*). Potatoes do well planted with beans, corn, cabbage and horseradish (which should be planted at the corners of a potato patch), marigold and eggplant (which is a lure for the Colorado potato beetle).

Potatoes do *not* do well near pumpkin, tomato, raspberry, squash and cucumber, and sunflower stunts its growth. The presence of these plants apparently lowers the potatoes' resistance to blight (*Phytophthora infestans*).

Irish Cobbler

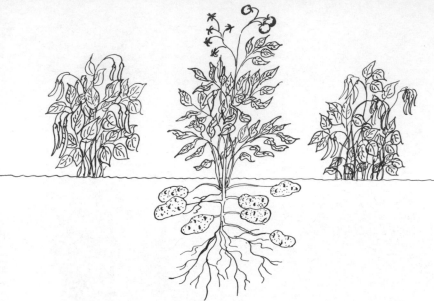

Bush beans grow well with potatoes as well as corn, cucumber, straw-berries, celery and summer savory. But keep onions away. Potatoes' other friends are corn, cabbage, marigold and horseradish. Don't plant them near cucumber, pumpkin, raspberries, squash, sunflowers or tomatoes. Eggplants planted nearby will lure the Colorado potato beetle.

Beans with potatoes protect against Colorado potato beetles and the potatoes protect the beans against Mexican bean beetle.

Horseradish or flax in rows between potatoes protects against the potato bug and the blister beetle. Flax improves both growth and flavor.

Nightshade weed (*Solanaceae*) attracts potato bugs, which eat the weed and die. Nightshade is a member of the same family as potatoes, has poisonous leaves, white flowers and black berries.

Hemp (*Cannabis*) grown in the neighborhood of potatoes helps protect against phytophthora infestans, the cause of late blight. Dead nettle, nasturtium and esparsette growing near are thought to be of benefit.

Potatoes do well when they follow a rye crop. Cabbages do well planted between potatoes after the first hilling. The presence of lamb's quarters in the potato patch is an indication that the crop should be moved to a new location.

Colorado potato beetles are attracted to eggplant, preferring it to the potatoes. A border grown around the potato patch will serve as a trap crop. Catch and destroy the beetles.

Potatoes should not be grown near orach or tomatoes, nor near apple trees, since the trees cause potatoes to be more susceptible to phytophthora blight.

Under light, potatoes develop a green color and an alkaloidal glucoside known as *solanine*, which is a poison. These potatoes should not be used for food unless all green is carefully removed. Ripening apples should not be stored in the same cellar as potatoes since they give off small amounts of ethylene gas which will give the potatoes an off flavor and affect their keeping quality. The apples, too, lose flavor in the presence of the potatoes.

Praying Mantis (*Mantidae*).   Despite its ferocious appearance this is one of our most beneficial insects, and it will not harm any vegetation in the garden, dining only on other insects. When young it eats the soft-bodied insects, the cutting and sucking aphids and leafhoppers; when fully mature it kills and eats chinch bugs, crickets, locusts, bees, wasps, beetles, flies, spiders, tent caterpillars and many others.

Though mantids usually are found in warm countries the common European mantid can live in the northern United States. A full-grown, large mantid varies from 2 to 5 inches in length depending on the kind, yet it will easily escape notice because in form and color it closely resembles the plants on which it rests.

Female mantids lay their eggs in masses, glueing them to trees and shrubs with a sticky substance from their bodies. The eggs remain there all winter, and if you carefully examine thorny bushes, brush, hedges and berry bushes in autumn after leaves have fallen, you may find the hardened froth mass egg cases. You can collect some from marshes and waste areas for your own garden, but never strip the area clean.

To place them properly, allow one egg case for each major shrub or about four for each quarter acre (without shrubbery). Select a sheltered spot and tie or tape the cases securely about two to four feet above the ground.

Early in the spring the mantis will start to aid you, emerging in

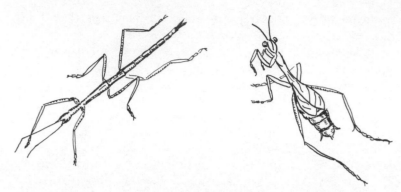

The praying mantis or walkingstick kills some good insects but rids a garden of many more injurious visitors.

bright sunshine usually from early May to late June, just at the time when a large variety of insect fare is likely to be available.

Each creature is fastened to the egg by a tenuous cord which it must break. After doing so it will drop and then climb to surrounding foliage. Mantids are poor flyers and slow movers and usually remain in the area as long as they continue to find food. And once introduced they are likely to multiply and extend control. Though many of the young may not live, still enough survive to perpetuate themselves. You can obtain mantid egg cases commercially, through the mail, usually between November and early May. (See SOURCES OF SUPPLY.)

Puffball (*Fungi*).   Sometimes these "smoke balls" or "devil's snuffboxes" grow to be more than two feet across. A cut that is bleeding profusely may be covered with the powder-like spores from those that produce a puff or "smoke" when disturbed, and it will stop the bleeding. Puffball powder is very explosive, so if you store it, keep the container closed and away from fire.

Pumpkin (*Cucurbita pepo*).   Pumpkins grow well when jimson weed (*datura*), sometimes called thorn apple, is in the vicinity. (See POISON PLANTS chapter.) Pumpkins grow well with corn, a practice followed by American Indians, yet pumpkins and potatoes have an inhibiting effect on each other.

Middle Eastern peoples consider the seeds an inexhaustible source of vigor offered by a bountiful nature. While we know today that there are no mysterious potions for tired lovers, we also know that some of the old formulas did perform seeming miracles —not through magic but through good nutrition—and pumpkin seeds are really vitamin-rich.

The variety *Tricky Jack* (Farmers), developed by the New Hampshire Experiment Station, has seeds which lack the shell of normal pumpkin and squash seeds, this "naked seed" being a genetic characteristic. *Tricky Jack* is a bush type and occupies little garden space. The hull-less seeds may be removed and simply washed and dried; they are a delicious snack when roasted and lightly salted.

Purslane *(Portulaca oleracea)*.   Purslane has a liking for good, cultivated soil and is frequently found in gardens. But it is not altogether unwelcome, for though often considered a weed, it is cultivated both in England and Holland. It is a refreshing green with a slightly acid taste, and it may be cooked like spinach. One hundred grams of purslane contains 3.5 milligrams of iron, more than any other plant except parsley, and this is all the more remarkable because the plant is 92.5 percent water.

Pyrethrum *(Chrysanthemum cinerariaefolium)*.   Pyrethrum is absolutely bugproof and will keep pests from plants close by. Few ticks are ever found where pyrethrum or sage form a ground cover. Pyrethrum powder, generally considered a safe insecticide, is made from the dried flowers. It has a very short residual action, breaking down rapidly in sunlight. Because of this it can be used as a pre-harvest spray. (See also FEVERFEW.)

Records show that pyrethrum may have been used nearly two thousand years ago in China. As an insect repellent it became popular again in the Nineteenth century and was the "secret ingredient" in Persian insect powder. In 1828 this powder was produced on a commercial scale and introduced into Europe by an

Armenian trader. By 1860 it was becoming well known in the United States. The active principles in pyrethrum are the esters, pyrethrin and cinerin.

Certain non-toxic plant products such as asarinin (from bark of southern prickly ash), sesamin (from sesame oil) and peperine (from black pepper), are added to pyrethrum to strengthen its effect.

Q

Quack Grass (*Agropyron repens* or *Triticum repens*). Quack grass indicates a crust formation and/or a hardpan in the soil. Choke it out by sowing millet, soybeans or cowpeas, making sure that the land first is thoroughly cultivated and the weather hot and dry. Two successive crops of rye also will choke it out.

A concentrated brine of common salt (sodium chloride) will kill it out, too, if used after grass is freshly cut and applied in dry weather several times. Dry weather will wilt the roots of quack grass, too, if they are brought to the surface. Hand-pulling is recommended if there are but a few plants.

Like so many other things quack grass isn't all bad. It is good cattle feed, and because of its persistence it makes a good covering for gullies and road banks where live soil has been cut open and few other plants will grow. Though hard to get rid of once it is started, it does prepare the soil for better things. Oddly, it is wheat's nearest relative. (See also GRASSES.)

R

Rabbit (*Oryctolagus cuniculus*). Onions are repellent to rabbits and may be interplanted with cabbage, lettuce, peas and beans. An old garden hose cut in lengths of a few feet each and arranged to look like snakes will frighten rabbits away.

Animal fat can be painted on young fruit trees, and a thin line of dried blood or blood meal sprinkled around the garden often acts as a repellent. Try a dusting of aloes on young plants or shake wood ashes, ground limestone or cayenne pepper on plants while they are wet with dew.

Raccoon (*Procyon lotor*). Farmers have been planting pumpkins and corn together for centuries to discourage raccoons. Put the pumpkin seeds about four feet apart, and as the corn approaches maturity the big, wide pumpkin leaves grow around the stalks. It is believed that the coons will not come into the corn rows because they like to be able to stand up and look around while they eat, and the big leaves make that impossible.

Other methods to control raccoons include sprinkling black or red pepper on the corn silks. This does not affect the taste of the corn. For a small planting, a wire "corn cage" or an electric fence

Repellants for the corn-loving raccoon include nearby cucumbers, melon, pumpkin or squash vines. Red or black pepper on the corn silk also may help.

is sure. If a six or 12-volt battery is used the fence will be harmless. It need be turned on only at night, since raccoons sleep during the day. Another solution is to use a small transistor radio (enclose in a plastic bag to protect from rain or dew), placing it in the patch at ripening time. Turn it on at night.

Radish (*Raphanus sativus*).   Radish is aided by redroot pigweed which loosens soil, and by nasturtiums and mustards' protective oils. Do not rotate radish with cabbage, cauliflower, Brussels sprout, kohlrabi, broccoli or turnip, since all are members of the cabbage family.

Early radishes are good to sow with beets, spinach, carrots and parsnips to mark the row. Sow radishes with cucumbers, squash and melons to repel the striped cucumber beetle, and with tomatoes to rout the two-spotted spider mite. Radishes grow well with kohlrabi, bush beans and pole beans. The presence of leaf lettuce in summer will make radishes more tender. Tobacco dust protects them from flea beetles and garlic juice from many diseases.

Radish and hyssop should never be sown near each other.

Ragweed (*Ambrosia artemisifolia*).   Whoever named this good-for-nothing weed "ambrosia," the food of the Greek gods, must have been playing a joke. Ragweeds produce pollen in great amounts and the wind distributes it to cause hay fever in those allergic to it. About 25 grains of pollen for each cubic yard are enough to cause the misery, and during the ragweed season when the plants bloom the air contains much more than this.

Unfortunately it will grow quickly in any untended spot. It is so ordinary looking, the flowers so inconspicuous, that so far efforts to eradicate it have failed. Mowing is recommended in midsummer to prevent production of pollen and seed.

Rape (*Brassica napus*).   Rape is an annual plant cultivated for its leaves and used as temporary pasture crop for livestock. Because of its deep taproot it loosens soil and improves drainage, leaving the land friable and ready to grow a more useful crop. It helps to heal soils injured by overdoses of mineral fertilizer.

The succulent rape grows fast, producing best under cool, moist conditions. It also resists rather severe frosts and is best seeded in the fall in the southern states and in the spring in the northern ones. Do not grow rape near hedge or field mustard since both will inhibit its growth.

Raspberry (*Rubus*).   If you grow both red and black raspberries put a considerable distance between the two types. The reason for this is that the reds sometimes carry a disease which does little or no harm to themselves but may prove near fatal to the blacks. Do not grow raspberries and blackberries near each other, either. Potatoes are more susceptible to blight if grown near raspberries, many gardeners believe.

Rattlebox (*Crotalaria*).   This weed is valuable for its soil-improving qualities, but one variety, *C. sagittalis,* found on bottomland in the Missouri and Mississippi basin, is very poisonous to cattle and horses and should be eradicated. Following its cutting or plowing under, plant a crop of cotton or corn which needs repeated cultivation.

Rhizobium.   These are the bacteria that form nodules on leguminous plants and turn atmospheric nitrogen into a useful form for building plant proteins. Unfortunately they withhold their talents from such useful plants as corn and wheat.

Researchers B. B. Bohlool and Edwin L. Schmidt at the University of Minnesota studying lectin, a plant protein that binds the saccharides on cell surfaces, experimentally bound it by means of a fluorescent dye to soybean seed. Then several rhizobia species were stained with the mixture to enable them to observe the binding of the lectin with the cells. It is their hope that in time they may effect a symbiotic relationship between rhizobium and a wide variety of other plants. More research is needed.

Rhubarb (*Rheum rhaponticum*).   This very ornamental as well

Rhubarb stems make delicious pies, but the leaves are very toxic and sometimes also cause skin irritation. They are safe on the compost pile, however.

as useful plant grown in flower beds is a good companion to columbines (*Aquilegia*), helping to protect them against red spider.

Rhubarb leaves, which contain oxalic acid, may be boiled in water and made into a spray which, watered into drillings before sowing brassicae, wallflowers and other seeds, is helpful in preventing clubroot. It is also useful on roses against greenfly and black spot.

Rhubarb, often called the "pie plant," is technically a vegetable but is mostly used for dessert. It also has been long recognized as a laxative. This is one of our oldest garden plants, which Marco Polo found growing in China centuries ago.

Rice, Wild (*Zizania aquatica*). This aquatic grass is not really rice at all nor is it related to rice. It grows from 4 to 8 feet tall in the shallow lakes of Minnesota, Wisconsin and central Canada where it is harvested by Indians who bend the heads of the plant over the edge of boats or canoes, beating the grains loose with two sticks.

Wild rice may be cultivated, growing best in quiet, pure water from one to six feet deep, along the margins of streams, ponds, lakes or the flood plains of rivers with rich mud bottoms. It likes a slow current and will not grow in stagnant lakes or pools. A fairly shallow farm pond fed by streams can provide a good supply of this vitamin B-rich delicacy.

Do not try to plant the product you find in the grocery store, for only unhulled seed will sprout. Rice for planting must be sacked and kept wet. The seed may be planted by scattering over the surface of the water at the rate of a bushel per acre. The good seed will sink rapidly. If your area is small, use a large handful to a six-by-six foot space. The best planting time is just before ice forms in late fall. For plants see SUPPLIERS INDEX.

Root Exudates. Roots of many crop and pasture plants have been found to excrete a vast variety of substances such as amino acids, vitamins, sugars, tannins, alkaloids, phosphates and many other unidentified substances. These have been found to be both helpful and inhibitory to plants growing near them. An experiment made with white pine tree seedlings, for instance, showed the presence of more than 35 different compounds of root excretions, including metabolites.

Root-knot. If the fresh tops of asparagus are crushed and steeped in water the solution may offer protection to vegetables where root-knot, stubby root and meadow nematodes are suspected. Marigolds are also useful against meadow nematodes.

Root Maggot.   Root maggots may be repelled by a mulch of oak leaves.

Roots.   Why do they go down? Hamed M. M. El-Antably and Paul Larsen of the University of Aarhus in Denmark believe that gibberellins (cell-elongating plant hormones) play a role in the downward growth behavior (geotropism) of roots.

Using the broad bean as an experiment they determined that as roots grow out horizontally from the young plant, the cell-elongating gibberellins accumulate in the upper portion of each root. These upper cells, being stimulated to elongate faster than the lower cells, cause the root to bend downward and grow toward the earth. After this bend occurs and the root starts growing vertically the gibberellic influence gradually lessens and cells on either side grow at about the same rate.

The roots of many plants, particularly weeds and grasses, are surprisingly and fortunately long, for the so-called "deep divers" bring up nutrients which the surface soil may lack, making it available in time to food plants. The total length of the root hairs of a single winter rye plant may be more than 5,000 miles!

Not all roots, however, go down as soil roots do. Some are aerial or air roots, such as poison ivy sometimes develops; others are water roots, such as water hyacinth and floating duckweed develop. Roots that get food from other plants, such as dodder and mistletoe are parasitic. They are companion plants we could do without.

Rosa Rugosa (*Rosa*). This "hippy" rose has become so famous that it deserves to be mentioned all by itself. Grown in a mass it makes a charming windbreak as well as an almost impenetrable barrier for animals. It blooms prolifically and is an excellent source

Rosa rugosa, often planted for a hedge, produces high-nutrient rose hips. It grows better with purslane, parsley and mignonette around it; is protected from rose bugs by alliums or onions nearby. Keep boxwood away.

for berries (hips) rich in vitamin C, containing more of this element than oranges. The hips are used for making teas, jams, soups and other dishes.

Roses (*Rosa*).   All the alliums—garlic, onions, chives and shallots —are beneficial to roses, protecting them against black spot, mildew and aphids. For a recipe to overcome black spot in roses see TOMATOES.

Garlic and onions are particularly beneficial to roses. In Bulgaria, where attar of roses is produced for perfumes, it is a common practice to interplant them with roses since they cause the roses to produce a stronger perfume in larger quantities.

Roses also are aided by the presence of parsley against rose beetles, onions to repel rose chafers, by mignonette as a ground cover and lupines to increase soil nitrogen and attract earthworms. Marigolds are helpful against nematodes, and geraniums or milky spore disease (See MILKY SPORE DISEASE) against Japanese beetle. A carpet of low-growing weeds from the purslane family among rosebushes will improve the spongy soil around their roots. An infusion of elderberry leaves in lukewarm water sprinkled over roses is thought to control caterpillar damage and is also recommended for blight.

Do not plant roses with other plants which have woody, outspreading roots that compete with the roses for soil nutrients.

Rubber Tree (*Hevea brasiliensis*).   What we call "the rubber tree," like citrus (to which it is protective) grows best in hot climates in deep, rich soils.

Rubber plant (*Ficus elastica* or *F. lyrata*), however, is the common name for a house plant related to the fig. This popular and attractive plant is known in its East Indian forest home as the "Assam Rubber Tree." It often begins life as an air plant, fixing its roots in the crotch of another tree, in which a chance seed has lodged. A shock of aerial roots strikes downward and reaches the ground, after which the tree depends upon food drawn from the earth.

Assam rubber, which ranks with the best Brazilian crude rub-

ber, comes from the sap of this wild fig tree. Rubber plants grown
in the house often are attacked by scale insects which may be destroyed by spraying the plant with nicotine. The more decorative
plant, *F. lyrata,* is not used for the production of commercial rubber.

Rue (*Ruta graveolens*).   By now I'm sure everybody knows that
rue doesn't like basil. But an authority as ancient as Pliny tells us
that "rue and the fig tree are in great league and amitie together."

Rue, planted near roses or raspberries will deter the Japanese
beetle. It can be clipped and made into an attractive hedge, but
first be sure you are not allergic to it, since the foliage can cause
dermatitis when the plant is coming into flower as severe as poison
ivy. The intensity of the eruption seems aggravated by the presence
of sunlight. If you happen to be perspiring and working bare-
handed with rue, you may get poisoned. If this happens washing
with brown soap or covering the exposed area with oil will help.

Rue may be grown among flowers as well as vegetables, where
its good looks will add to the planting. It is protective to many
trees and shrubs. It is good near manure piles and around barns
for discouraging both house and stable flies.

The ancient, Schola Salernitans, wrote that "Rue putteth fleas
to flight." However, it should be used only for dog pillows or beds,
for cats do not like it. Anything rubbed with the leaves of rue will
be free from cats' depredations—good to know if your house cats
tend to claw the furniture.

Rye (*Secale cereale*).   Rye is an excellent crop to choke out chickweed and other low-growing weeds that survive the winter. Planted
twice in succession it even will choke out quack grass. A cover crop
following sod will reduce black spot on strawberries and pink root
on onions.

Rye will be benefitted by cornflowers in the ratio of 100 to 1,
while a few pansies in the field will aid it, and the wild pansy
(*viola*) will germinate almost 100 percent if grown near by. Rye
has an inhibiting effect on field poppy, retarding both the germination of the seed and its growth.

Rye flour sprinkled over cabbage plants while they are wet with morning dew will dehydrate cabbageworms and moths. Refined diatomaceous earth is useful as an insecticide for stored rye, but it is not injurious to warm-blooded animals.

S

Sage (*Salvia officinalis*).   Sage is protective to cabbages and all their relatives against the white cabbage butterfly, and it also makes the cabbage plants more succulent and tasty.

The herb also is good to grow with carrots, protecting them against the carrot fly, and is mutually beneficial with rosemary. Do not plant sage with cucumber, which does not like aromatic herbs in general and sage in particular.

Originally sage was used medicinally in stuffing and meats to make them more digestible, but we have grown to like the flavor and do not realize we are taking an herbal remedy.

Sage tea is made from a half ounce of chopped fresh sage leaves, one ounce of sugar, the juice of 1/2 lemon and 1 teaspoonful of grated lemon rind. Pour over this a quart of boiling water and allow to infuse for half an hour, straining before use. This tea, is good for both people and plants. The plants, however, must take it cold.

Salsify (*Tragopogon porrifolius*).   Sometimes this is called oyster plant. To achieve a delicate and different flavor the milky oyster-flavored roots need a moist, cool soil for at least four months before reaching maturity.

Salsify grows well with mustard greens, and try growing it with watermelons. Plant the warm-weather watermelon several weeks later than the cool-weather salsify. Let the melons fill the middles of the rows before hot, dry weather arrives. Acting as a living mulch and tending to rest on the ground, the melon vines still will leave the salsify foliage exposed to light and air.

Never use salsify seed over a year old.

Salt, Common (*Sodium chloride*).　Salt has a damaging effect on most plants and should not be used except where the soil is to be rested for a time afterwards. It is useful to kill Canada thistle or quack grass and will give best results if put on after the weeds are freshly cut. Apply several times, taking care to do so only in dry weather. Salt put on slugs will dissolve them.

Salt Herbs.　The clever use of herbs can replace salt in many dishes and reduce the amount needed in others. Those on a salt-free diet can flavor their food deliciously by using such herbs as celery, summer savory, thyme, lovage and marjoram.

Santolina (*Chamaecyparis*).　This South European plant, sometimes called lavender cotton, is a good moth repellent. The name is from *Sanctum linum,* meaning "holy flax." The plants are improved by being pruned as soon as the blossoms fall.

Saponin.　Soapberry or chinaberry is the name of a group or genus of trees and shrubs that bear fruit containing a soapy substance called saponin. Bouncing Bet is probably our best known saponin-rich plant. Other unrelated plants such as primroses and carnations also have this quality, as well as many legumes, cyclamen tubers, camellia, labiates, horse chestnut, orach, pokeweed, runner beans, tomatoes, mullein, potatoes and viola. These plants are important because their decomposing remains create a favorable environment for the plants that come after them.

Commercial saponin is used as a foam-producer in beverages and fire extinguishers and also as a detergent useful in washing delicate fabrics.

Sassafras (*Sassafras albidum*).　Traps baited with sassafras oil are a good control for the codling moth. Here is how to make a solid bait: Fill a small ice cream cup two-thirds full of sawdust, stir into it a teaspoon of sassafras oil and a tablespoon of glacial acetic acid. Add enough glue to thoroughly saturate the mixture. In a day or two, when the cup is dry, suspend it in a mason jar partly filled with water. It works very well placed in fruit trees.

Bark from the sassafras or "mitten" tree makes a delicious drink.

Sassafras also will repel mosquitoes. The pungent oil has antiseptic properties, and the bark mixed with dried fruit wards off insects.

A delicious tea made from the bark of young sassafras roots (best if sweetened with honey) is considered helpful for digestive disturbances. The dried leaves, called "file," are much used in the southern states as an ingredient in soups.

Sassafras is sometimes called "the mitten tree" from its peculiar leaves which grow in three different shapes: the simple ovate leaf, a larger blade (oval in form but with one side extended and lobed to form a thumb) and thirdly, a symmetrical three-lobed leaf, the pattern of a narrow mitten with a thumb on each side.

Savory, Summer (*Satureia hortensis*).   In Germany savory is called "the bean herb" because it's good to grow with beans and also to cook with them. It goes with onions as well, improving both growth and flavor.

Savory, Winter (*Satureia montana*).   Winter savory is a sub-shrub about 15 inches tall. Its leaves, though not as delicate as summer savory, may be used in cooking. It is useful as an insect repellent, too.

Sawdust Mulch.   There is much to be said about a sawdust mulch, both "for" and "against." Mulches like sawdust are particularly susceptible to spontaneous combustion, fresh sawdust can cause a depletion in soil nitrogen, and it is not good to use in summer because earthworms will avoid it.

On the good side, it is claimed by many authorities that blueberries, mulched with sawdust will develop a larger, more fibrous root system and as an end result have a far higher yield. It is considered good mulch for raspberries and should be put on immediately after transplanting. Mixed with animal manures or poultry litter it makes an acceptable mulch for many plants and shrubs where either one alone would not work well.

The type of tree from which the sawdust comes also has a bearing on the situation. Unweathered pine sawdust will decompose very slowly, so give it a bit of time to weather and turn gray before using. Sawdust from hardwood trees will rot much more rapidly than either pine or spruce or cedar, especially if weathered before using.

As mentioned previously, "cutting" or mixing sawdust with other materials is a good idea. It should be mentioned also that studies now show that the tannins and terpenes in sawdust which gardeners often fear, really do little if any harm to the soil. Shavings or sawdust used for animal bedding make an excellent mulch. (See *The Mulch Book* in SUGGESTED READING.)

Sea Onion, Squill (*Urginea maritima*).   Squills have a history of medicinal usage dating back about 4000 years to the Egyptian Ebers Papyrus, which lists as a remedy for heart troubles a "prescription" including the bulbs of squills. Hippocrates, Theophrastus and Dioscorides, as well as Pliny all had much to say about squills, most of it wrong. From their day to the present the squill has been used in the preparation of medicines and also as an ornamental in our gardens.

Various cardioactive, diuretic and emetic glycosides—scillitoxin, scillipicrin, scillin to mention but a few—have been isolated from the squill bulb, which may grow as large as four pounds.

A preparation made from squill is useful for colic in cattle, but should be used only under the direction of a veterinarian for it can be poisonous. Indeed red squill powder is manufactured as a poison for rodents.

Urginea belongs to the lily family, Liliacea, whose name is derived from an Arabic tribe in Algeria which probably was the first to use the bulbs medicinally.

Seaweed.   Kelps, a type of brown algae, provide fertilizer and are a source of the chemical element iodine, particularly the giant kelps of the Pacific. Chemists also extract from kelps large amounts of algin which is useful in such commercial products as ice cream and salad dressings by virtue of its ability to hold several different liquids together.

Kelp is about 20 to 25 percent potassium chloride, and it also contains common salt, sodium carbonate, boron, iodine and other trace elements. For gardeners who live on or near the seacoast, seaweeds are a natural and usually wasted resource which can be utilized for mulching and in compost piles. They are especially good materials to put around fruit trees. Another advantage is that decomposing seaweed is less attractive to mice than straw.

Chopping seaweed may be advantageous if only for cosmetic reasons. Also it may be advisable to rinse off the salt, but it is not necessary to be too fussy about this. The small amount left clinging will do no harm. Eelgrass, which dries into a light "hay" and doesn't pack down, is a perfect non-smothering material for many plants. (See EELGRASS.)

Another use for "sea power" to promote fertility is liquified seaweed, which may be applied as a foliar fertilizer directly to the leaves of plants, being particularly helpful to trees.

It has been found that seaweed as a fertilizer helps to promote frost resistance in tomatoes and citrus fruits, along with increasing the sweetness in some fruits and giving better resistance to pests and diseases. Beets and parsnips respond badly to boron shortages in the soil, so chopped kelp makes an excellent mulch for them.

Eelgrass makes an enriching mulch, is fine for composting.

Seaweed helps to break down certain insoluable elements in the soil, making them available to plants. This quickens seed germination and further aids development of blossoms and fruits, resulting in increased yields.

For those who cannot readily obtain seaweed there is fish emulsion, available at most garden centers and through nursery catalogs (*Parks*). Another idea for gardeners who, like myself, live far inland, is water plants. Though not as rich as seaweeds, they make good mulch if chopped, and are good additions to the compost. Water hyacinth, a plant of tropical America, has escaped into the wild and has become a pest, choking many small streams. Dredged from waterways, it is valuable on the mulch pile. Here where I live water lilies grow profusely in shallow pools and are easily obtainable. My husband Carl and I usually bring back a tubful of water weeds of some kind every time we go fishing.

Sesame (*Sesamum orientale*).   Sesame is an herb grown in tropical countries, mainly for the oil obtained from its seeds. The oil is used in salad dressings and for cooking, while the delicious seeds are used to flavor bread, candy, biscuits and other delicacies.

Sesame is very sensitive to root exudates from sorghum (*Andropogon sorghum*) and will not ripen well when grown near it. Sesamin is derived from sesame oil and is used as a synergist to strengthen the effect of pyrethrum.

Shade.   Shade is sometimes the decisive factor in companion planting. Nature does not arrange plants in long, straight rows as we often do in our gardens. Try radishes in a foot-wide bed with no thinning. Put fast-growing lettuce such as buttercrunch, simpson or oakleaf, between cabbages, broccoli, Brussels sprouts or even tomatoes, which will shade the young plants while they are growing. The lettuce will be up and out of the way when the slower-maturing plants need the room. You'll have a double crop on half the ground and with half the work, and you will also find the brassicas giving the lettuce just enough shade to keep it coming on crisp and sweet right into hot weather.

If you interplant early beets with late potatoes the shade of the growing potatoes will benefit the beets, keeping them tender and succulent right into warm weather.

Plant melons between your onion rows and by the time the onions are harvested the melons will be taking over the ground. While the vines are growing the onions will protect them from insects.

After you harvest your early corn let the stalks remain a while to shade a planting of fall cabbage, beans, peas and turnips. When the fall garden is well established and the sun less warm, remove the cornstalks and use them for mulch right on the ground where they grew.

Many of the mints take kindly to shade and may be grown under trees. Sweet woodruff also likes shade and makes an excellent ground cover, while retaining moisture for other plants which give it protection from the sun. Tarragon and chervil like partial shade, too.

Shallot (*Allium ascalonicum*).   Shallots, more delicate in flavor than onions, are propagated by planting the sections or cloves of which the large bulb consists. They are good to grow with most garden vegetables but, like onions and garlic, should not be located near peas or beans.

Shepherd's Purse (*Capsella Bursa-pastoris*).   Dr. Eldon L. Reeves, an insect pathologist at the University of California, found that seeds of both shepherd's purse and *Lepidum flavum* trap mosquito larvae with a natural glue which forms a coating when the seed is immersed in water. During feeding, the larvae come in contact with the seed, are stuck fast by their mouth-brushes and die. It is considered advisable to sterilize the seed by heat before using them this way so they will not germinate.

Shepherd's purse is very rich in minerals. Along with mustard it absorbs excessive salts in the soil and returns them in organic form. If grown on a salty marsh and plowed under while still green, it will both sweeten the soil and also take away the life element of the weeds ordinarily growing on such soil. It has medicinal qualities and has been used as a styptic.

Silica.   Silicic acid, one of the minerals, can be found in many plants such as stinging nettle, quack or couch grass, but there are some such as horsetail (*Equisetum arvense*) and knotweed (*Polygonum aviculare*), which are particularly rich in it. It is this silica in horsetail which has made it valuable medicinally for centuries.

Silicic acid strengthens tissue, particularly that of the lungs, and at times adds to disease resistance. It has been reported to have a good influence on inflammation of the gums, the mouth or the skin in general.

A tea made of horsetail is very effective against mildew and other fungi found on fruit tress, grapevines, vegetables and roses. It is gentle but swift in action and does not disturb soil life.

According to Beatrice Trum Hunter, silica in the form of an aerogel is one of our most effective insecticides. It may be used against the flour beetle, rice weevil, granary weevil and the larva of the Mediterranean flour moth.

In German-speaking countries horsetail was called *Zinnkraut* or "pewter plant" because the high silica content made it useful for cleaning and scrubbing copper, brass, pewter and all fine metals.

Horsetail was specially recommended for diuretic purposes by Kneipp, the South German priest who was so successful in using hydrotherapy in connection with herbs. Silica-rich plants are valuable on the compost pile, too.

Slugs and Snails (*Agriolimax campestris* and *Helicidae*).   These beasties cause most of their damage at night in places where the ground is damp. They are topers, love beer and will drown in saucers of it. Even empty beer cans placed in the garden attract them by their odor. Snails are reluctant to cross lines of ashes or hydrated lime, but they love honey and will drown in saucers of that. What a way to go!

Since ordinary table salt will dissolve slugs, I find it handy to carry a small salt shaker in my pocket to use when I spot them. I feel no compunction, for these slimy creatures will destroy my choicest cabbage and lettuce heads if they get a chance.

Tobacco stem meal discourages slugs, and white hellebore controls them on grapes and cherries. They dislike tanbark or oak leaves, and either wormwood or quassia will repel them by its bitterness.

Sorghum (*Andropogon sorghum*) (*S. vulgare* or *Holcus sorghum*). Several insect-resistant strains of sorghum have been developed: *Atlas* is resistant to the chinch bug, while *Milo* is susceptible; *Sudan* is resistant to the corn leaf aphid, while *White Martin* is susceptible.

The sweet sorghums or sorgos are grown especially for the production of sorghum syrup which is made by pressing the juice out of the stems. For the gardener who would like to be self-sufficient, here is a source of sweetening for his other foods. To get the maximum amount of sugar in the juice, sorghum should be seeded on soils that are not too fertile. Large vigorous stalks usually are lower in sugar than those grown more slowly and which are not over a half-inch in diameter.

Root exudates of sorghum apparently are poisonous to sesame and wheat. Stored sorghum grain can be kept free of insects by refined diatomaceous earth used as a desiccant dust.

Southernwood (*Artemisia abrotanum*).   Dry the leaves of southernwood, place them in nylon net bags and hang them in the closet to prevent moths. Burned to ashes in the fireplace they will remove any cooking odors from the house.

Southernwood has green, finely-divided leaves with a lemon-mixed-with-pine scent. Grown near cabbages it will protect them from cabbage worm butterfly and near fruit trees, will repel fruit tree moths. Among its names are "old man," "lad's love," and even "maidens' ruin"!

Sow Thistle (*Sonchus arvensis*).   This plant has creeping, deep-growing roots, contains a milky, yellow-tinged juice and grows on moist soil. It aids watermelon, muskmelon, pumpkin and cucumber and in moderate amounts onions, tomatoes and corn.

A cousin called blessed thistle (*Cnicus benedictus*) has medicinal and industrial uses and is a basic ingredient of the Benedictine liqueur as well as certain bitter tonics.

Soya Bean—Soybean (*G. soya* and *Glycine max*).   Soya beans, native of China, are so rich in protein they have been called the "meat without a bone." Like all legumes they loosen and enrich

Soybeans, like all legumes, enrich the soil. They grow faster and thicker than weeds and will choke them out.

poor soil and are an excellent crop to grow preceding others that need nitrogen.

Soybeans planted near corn protect it against chinch bugs and Japanese beetles. They grow well with black-eye peas and will choke out weeds because they grow so rapidly.

They are perhaps the world's oldest food crop, and they have meant meat, milk, cheese, bread and oil to the Asiatic peoples for centuries.

Spearmint (*Mentha spicata*).   Spearmint also is called "green mint," "pea mint" and "lamb mint." (See also MINT.)

Spider (*Arachnida*).   Some mites and spiders are natural predators, our valuable allies which dine on many destructive insects. One type of predaceous mite is used to control plant-feeding insects on avocado and citrus crops.

The garden spider is one of the best helpers to the vegetable grower.

Spider Mite (*Acarina*).   Spider mites sometimes can be removed from plants by spraying forcibly with a stream of plain water, and once dislodged from a plant they seldom return. A 3 percent oil spray, pyrethrum dust, or a spray of onions and hot peppers may be used, and I have found that garlic will repel the mites on tomato plants, while ladybugs are their natural enemies. Spider mites, also called "red spider," are apt to show up suddenly in hot weather.

Spinach (*Spinacia oleracea*).   Because of its saponin content spinach is a useful pre-crop and does well planted with strawberries. Bacillus thuringiensis may be used as an insect control.

Sprays.   In using most sprays made from botanicals it is a good idea to add a small amount of real soap to help the materials adhere. Washing plants down with just plain soapy water is an excellent practice in many instance, for soap appears to have antiseptic qualities useful against many plant diseases.

Spruce (*Picea*).   Three species of woodpeckers were credited with controlling a serious infestation of spruce beetles in Colorado in 1947. Naturally-occurring bacillus thuringiensis has been found to give good control of this beetle in some forests.

Spurge (*Euphorbia lathyrus* and *E. lactea*).   Injury to stem or leaves of the euphorbias cause them to exude a milky-looking sap that is very acrid and poisonous. Great care should be taken that the sap does not touch a scratch, as it will even cause blisters on delicate skin.

Snow-on-the-mountain, one of the euphorbias, is an attractive annual plant which grows wild from Minnesota to Texas. Poinsettia is another lovely but poisonous member of this family.

If your garden is troubled by moles try planting the spurges. They also are called "mole plants," for moles dislike them, and they also are useful to repel rats and mice.

Squash (*Curcubitaceae*).   Two or three icicle radishes planted in each hill will help prevent insects on squash as on cucumbers. Let

& calendulas

the radishes grow and go to seed. Nasturtiums will repel squash bugs and so will cigarette ash and other tobacco residue if placed with the seed when it is planted. Squash planted either earlier or later than usual often will escape insect damage. I find fall-planted squash almost entirely insect-free.

Early in the day before the sun is strong, squash stinkbugs are sluggish, and in the small garden may be picked off. There also are insect-resistant strains of squash. (See INSECT-RESISTANT VEGE-TABLES AND GRAINS.)

Stinging Nettle (*Urtica dioica*).   Among stinging nettle's helpful qualities, it makes neighboring plants more insect-resistant. It also helps plants withstand lice, slugs and snails during wet weather, strengthens growth of mint and tomatoes, and gives greater aromatic quality to herbs such as valerian, anglica, marjoram, sage and peppermint. The nettle also slows fermentation, keeps fruit

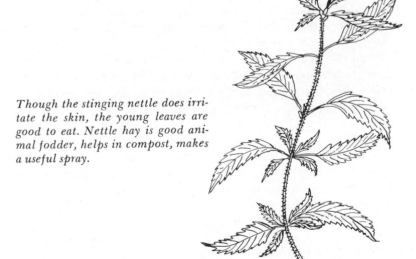

Though the stinging nettle does irritate the skin, the young leaves are good to eat. Nettle hay is good animal fodder, helps in compost, makes a useful spray.

mold free and thus enables it to keep better. Fruit packed in nettle hay ripen more quickly. Stinging nettle is helpful to stimulate fermentation in compost or manure piles, according to British author M. E. Bruce, who advises making a crushed nettle solution.

Good results can be had with less trouble by using the nettle in its original form, placing it in layers in the compost before the nettle seeds ripen. The plant is said to contain carbonic acid and ammonia which may be the factors which activate the compost. If you have the space you might try raising a crop of nettle—somewhere away from the garden, for the plant spreads quickly.

Euell Gibbons reports that stinging nettle combined with young horseradish leaves are delicious as spring greens. It also combines well with lettuce or spinach.

Since nettles are rich in vitamins and iron they are a good remedy for anemia, while aiding blood circulation and acting as a stimulant. The plant leaves, as rich in protein as cottonseed meal, are good for animals, too, though they will touch them only when mowed and dried. Horses improve in health and cows will give more and richer milk. When powdered nettle leaves are added to their mash, hens will lay more eggs and the eggs will have a higher food value, chicks will grow faster and turkeys will fatten. Even the manure from nettle-fed animals is better than that from others.

Be sure to wear gloves when picking young nettles, for the fine hairs on the leaves and stems contain formic acid, which irritates the skin when touched. Nettle rash can be relieved with the juice of the nettle plant itself, or by rubbing the skin with jewelweed, with rhubarb or any member of the sorrel family.

St. John's Wort (*Hypericum perforatum*).   This common pasture plant contains a red oil sometimes used as a home remedy for bronchitis and chest colds. It also is astringent and has been used against diarrhea and dysentery. The leaves have oily cells and a strong, peculiar smell. They look perforated if held against the light. It was once believed that if the plant was collected during St. John's Night (June 24th), it would afford protection against witches and evil spirits.

Strawberry (*Fragaria*). A cover crop of rye following sod will reduce the incidence of black rot on strawberries. They do well in combination with bush beans, spinach and borage. Lettuce is good used as a border and pyrethrum, planted alongside, serves well as a pest preventative. A spruce hedge also is protective.

White hellebore will control sawfly and marigolds are useful too if you suspect the presence of nematodes. Pine needles alone or mixed with straw make a fine mulch said to make the berries taste more like the wild variety. Spruce needles also may be used as a mulch, but my personal preference is chopped alfalfa hay.

For cultural directions on strawberries and other berries see in SUGGESTED READING *The Complete Guide to Growing Berries and Grapes.*

Succession Planting. This will enable you to make the most of a supply of compost or fertilizer. Heavy feeders such as broccoli, Brussels sprouts, cabbage, cauliflower, celeriac, celery, chard, cucumber, endive, kohlrabi, leek, lettuce, spinach, squash, sweet corn and tomato should be planted in soil newly fertilized with well-decomposed manure.

Follow these heavy feeders with light feeders such as beet, carrot, radish, rutabaga and turnip which also like finely-pulverized raw rocks and compost.

Legumes, the third group in succession planting, include broad and lima beans, bush and pole beans, pea and soybean. These are the soil improvers which collect nitrogen on their roots and restore it to the soil.

Sudan Grass (*Sorghum vulgare sudanense*). This is a tall annual sorghum whose thin stalks grow quickly and may reach a height of ten feet. It serves as excellent summer pasturage, grows well with soybeans if sufficient moisture is present.

Johnson grass, a perennial sorghum, grows as a weed in the southern United States. It resembles Sudan grass but spreads by creeping rootstocks in gardens or on land needed for cotton or other row crops to become a pest, but it makes excellent hay for cattle feed.

Sugar and Herbs.   Three herbs which can reduce the use of sugar in cooking and sweets are lemon balm, sweet cicely and angelica, particularly good in tart fruit or fruit pies made of black currant, red currant, rhubarb, gooseberry, plums and tart apples. Not only do these herbs make it possible to use sometimes half the usual quantity of sugar, but they also impart a delicious flavor. Chopped sweet cicely may be added to lightly-sugared strawberries.

Sugar Beet (*Beta vulgaris*).   Grain can be partially replaced as stock feed by sugar beets, which are liked by all animals and are good for increasing the milk flow of cows. Cheat grass is often a despised weed but has the ability to quickly form a ground cover over denuded soil, preventing erosion. At the same time it replaces plants that are host to beet leafhopper, making it of considerable importance to sugar beet growers.

Suicide in Plants.   Why do most annual plants die in the autumn? Larry D. Nooden and Susan L. Schreyer at the University of Michigan are studying a chemical "death signal," possibly a hormone, which they have traced to plant seeds. The possibility is being considered that seeds inside mature fruits such as soybean pods send out hormones, which cause plants to yellow and die even before nights cold enough for freezing cut them down.

Gardeners for years have known that if faded flowers are picked before they form seeds the plants will continue to produce more flowers. Pansies are a good example. Among the vegetables okra will continue from early spring to frost if the pods are kept picked before they harden.

Nooden says that this idea was tested on soybeans. Growing pods were plucked from one side of the plant only and allowed to remain on the other. The side with the mature pods and seeds turned yellow and died, the other remained healthy.

Sunflower (*Helianthus annuus*).   Sometimes called "maiz de Texas" (Texas corn) or "tourne-soleil," the common sunflower is an American plant which has been widely cultivated and much improved. And it is itself a soil improver when grown in moderation

Sunflowers are good companions to cucumbers, but not to potatoes or pole beans.

through certain farm crops. However, sunflower seeds will not germinate well where grass was growing in close proximity, Dr. Edgar Anderson has discovered.

Sunflowers are now believed to produce leaf substances which inhibit other species. E. L. Rice at the University of Oklahoma attributes this to a defense mechanism of the plant. Needing little nitrogen itself, the sunflower produces a substance which inhibits nitrogen-fixing bacteria in the soil, thus delaying the day when grasses and other succeeding plants may take over. According to Rice the sunflower leaves a zone of "little growth" around itself. Sunflowers and potatoes have an inhibiting effect on each other that results in both being stunted. Potatoes also are more likely to be infected by phytophthora blight.

Sunflowers and pole beans should not be planted together since both compete for space and light with resulting poor growth. It has been found that corn and sunflowers are protective to each other and insects are reduced on each. (See CORN.)

Sunflowers have their good points as well, and cucumbers benefit when sunflowers are grown near them to provide a windbreak. In my hot climate I grow sunflowers on the west side of the cucumber patch to provide shade in the afternoon. Both cucumbers and sunflowers like a rich soil, so I dig in plenty of compost to prevent one from starving out the other.

Sunflowers not only can provide a windbreak but a quick-growing screen for any portion of the garden where visibility is undesirable—a compost heap for instance. Their blooms are visited by bees for pollen and nectar and the seeds, which are loved by birds, are rich in vitamins B_1, A, D and F, and make a fine vegetable oil for cooking and salad dressings.

Sweet Basil (*Ocimum basilicum*).   Basil is a good companion for tomatoes, improving flavor and growth, but it dislikes rue intensely. It repels mosquitoes and flies, and when laid over tomatoes in a serving bowl will deter fruit flies.

Though it is often said that herbs enhance everything except dessert, sweet basil is one that may be used to give a subtle, indefinable but delicious flavor to pound cake. It is also one of the culinary herbs that may be used in certain dishes to replace black pepper, of value to people who have digestive problems yet enjoy pepper as a flavoring. (See PEPPER, HERBS USED.)

Sweet Clover (*Melilotus alba* and *M. Indica*).   This is not a true clover although it is a legume. White and yellow sweet clovers live for two years, and their large roots penetrate deeply into the soil. At the end of the second season they decay to enrich the soil with nitrogen and decomposing vegetable material.

Sour clover, a kind of sweet clover used almost entirely to improve the soil, is often called melilot.

Spoiled sweet clover hay or poorly-preserved silage never should be fed to animals. The hay contains *coumarin,* an anticoagulant, which develops toxicity as the clover decomposes and thus it may cause both internal and external bleeding.

Sweet Potato (*Ipomea batalas*).   *Nemagold* sweet potatoes developed by the Oklahoma Experiment Station have built-in resistance to nematodes. Sweet potatoes generally have high energy value, only peas and beans yielding more. They have a common enemy, the fungus disease or wilt called "stem rot" which can be controlled with disease-free seed and by rotating the crop. White hellebore controls a number of leaf-eating insects.

If rabbits bother your sweet potato patch spray with a diluted fish emulsion. (Parks has one called Mer-Made Fish Emulsion.)

Sycamore (*Platanus occidentalis*).   Studies conducted by American and Iraqi scientists show that sycamores inhibit the growth of other herbaceous plant species, and the decaying leaves cause significant reduction in seed germination and seedling growth. Organic compounds leached from the leaves often are allelopathic to plants, and virtually no herbaceous plants will grow under the trees.

Sycamore bark has value, however. Boiled in water and made into a poultice, it is good to use for poison ivy.

Symbiosis.   Symbiosis means the living together in intimate association or even union, of two dissimilar organisms. A common example are the lichens, which are really double plants, a combination of a fungus and an alga living together, each deriving benefit from the other.

Another example is the yucca plant and the yucca moth. One cannot exist without the other. Pollination is possible for the yucca only with the help of the moth. The moth larvae, on the other hand, cannot survive without the food provided by the flower, yet there always are enough seeds left so that the plant can survive.

Antibiosis is the opposite of symbiosis, as is antipathetic symbiosis. This means that the association, as in parasitism, is disadvantageous or destructive to one of the organisms—mistletoe as an example.

Tansy (*Tanacetum vulgare*). Tansy is considered dangerous if taken as an infusion, (see chapter on POISONOUS PLANTS). But planted under fruit trees, particularly peach, it repels borers, and is a good companion to roses, raspberries, blackberries, grapes and other cane fruits. It deters flying insects, Japanese beetles, striped cucumber beetles and squash bugs, helps repel flies and ants. The dried leaves are useful for storing woolens and furs.

Tansy also goes by the names of bitter buttons, ginger plant, hind heal, and scented fern. Its fern-like, attractive foliage is topped by composite heads of button-like flowers, and their scent is delightful. Though the roots have been used, it is the tops that are of primary importance.

Tansy once was used as a culinary herb in place of pepper, was widely used in churches in medieval times as a "strewing herb," and was one of the plants associated with the Virgin Mary.

The plant contains volatile oil, wax, stearine, chlorophyll, bitter resin, yellow coloring matter, tannin and gallic acid, bitter extractive gum and tanacetic acid (which is crystallizable) and precipi-

Plant tansy in orchards and the garden to deter borders and flying insects. It once was used as a medicinal tea but now is considered poisonous to humans and to cattle.

tated lime, baryta and oxide of lead. Because of its concentration
of potassium, tansy is useful on the compost pile.

Tarragon, French (*Artemisia dracunculus*).   Use potato fertilizer
as a side dressing for tarragon in the spring and again right after
the first cutting to increase the vitality of the plant. To reset tarragon successfully the roots must be carefully untangled. Each sec-
tion of root eased apart from the clump may be reset to form another plant. This is best done every third year in March or early
April. As a cooking herb tarragon is something very special, and
it is particularly good for flavoring vinegar.

Tea Leaves.   Mix tea leaves with radish and carrot seed to prevent
maggots.

Termite (*Termitidae*).   Since most termites cannot live without
water, cutting off the source of moisture usually kills them. Silica
aerogel is effective and extracts of chinaberry will kill about 98
percent of them.

Thistle (*Circium*).   All thistles are rich in potassium and thus are
useful in compost. But their prickly leaves make them unpopular
in pastures, and certain types rob grain fields of food and moisture.
To kill out thistles be careful not to cut them before the blossoms
are open or many more will grow from the rootstocks. If you cut
just the blossom-heads after the blossoms are pollinated, the plant
will bleed to death and die.

Blessed thistle (*Cnicus benedictus*) has medicinal and industrial
uses, as well as being an insect repellent, while constituting a basic
ingredient of the Benedictine liqueur and stomach bitters.

Thorn Apple (*Datura stramonium*).   See DATURA.

Thyme (*Thymus vulgaris*).   Thyme has an ancient history as a
medicinal and culinary herb. The oil still is used as the basis of a
patent cough medicine, while thymol has anti-bacterial powers of

considerable importance. But thyme is of value mainly in cooking, being very good for poultry seasoning and dressing. Lemon thyme makes a delicious herbal tea.

The herb deters the cabbage worm and is good planted anywhere in the garden, accenting the aromatic qualities of other plants and herbs.

Tillandsia (*T. usneoides*). Tillandsia (also called Spanish moss, though not a true moss), occurs naturally from Virginia to Florida and Texas and southward to Argentina and Chili. Though it may be seen on other trees its favorite host is the live oak. It is not a parasite, sapping the life of the tree, but a lodger that finds its own food supply through slender, grayish stems which look like hair hanging from the trees. It is related to the air plants of the bromelia or pineapple family which largely draw their sustenance from the air itself. It may be used for mulching or for compost. The dried stems also are used industrially to stuff upholstery.

Timothy (*Phleum pratense*). Timothy and other small grains are benefitted by planting them with legumes such as alfalfa and sweet clover as a protection against white grubs. Timothy, a valuable, cool-season grass perennial, sometimes called herd's grass and by the English cat's-tail, has slender stems bearing round spikes of tiny, tightly-packed flowers. Farmers in both Canada and the United States often sow timothy in rotation with oats and other grains. It does not last long when cattle or other animals graze on it continually, and is not considered a satisfactory pasture grass unless mixed with hardier types.

Toad (*Bufo*). Both toads and frogs consume many insects, one toad being able to eat up to 10,000 insects in three months' time—and many of these will be cutworms. Other insects eaten by toads include crickets, grubs, rose chafers, rose beetles, caterpillars, ants, squash bugs, sow (pill) bugs, potato beetles, moths, mosquitoes, flies, slugs and even moles.

Toads do *not* cause warts and are not poisonous to man, though they exude a slime distasteful to their enemies. If you want to

Horned toads, like other varieties, are great friends of the gardener, devouring great numbers of insects. Help them find shelter in your garden area.

secure some toads for your garden, look around the edges of swamps and ponds in spring. Once secured they need shelter and a source of water. A clay flowerpot with a small hole broken out of the side will serve for housing if buried a few inches in the ground in a shady place. They also need a shallow pan of water and, if your garden is not fenced, protection from dogs and other crea-tures.

In the Southwest, we use the horned toads (really a lizard) in the same way. They can withstand more heat and thrive in my garden, apparently living on dew and insects. They bury them-selves in the ground during winter, emerging when the weather warms up.

Tobacco (*Nicotiana tabacum*).   Ever since the late Seventeenth century tobacco and its main alkaloid, nicotine, have been used for insecticidal purposes. In a pure state this is a colorless fluid with little odor, but it is a virulent poison for insects and highly toxic to animals. It is, however, volatile, dissipating readily from plants on which it is sprayed or dusted. It is useful against soft-bodied insects such as aphid, white fly, leafhopper, psylla, thrip and spider mite. Dried, ground tobacco added to a suspension of bentonite in water has been found useful to spray on apple trees against codling moths.

Tobacco likes to be fertilized with a compost made from its own leaves, and it prefers to grow in the same place year after year. The leaf of tobacco is poisonous due to the nicotine content.

Tomato (*Lycopersicon esculentum*).   Tomatoes will protect asparagus against the asparagus beetle. Since they are tender plants, put tomatoes in during late spring after the early crop of asparagus spears have been harvested. Tomatoes and all members of the Brassica family grow well together, the tomatoes repelling the white cabbage butterfly. They also protect gooseberries against insects.

Tomatoes are compatible with chives, onion, parsley, marigold, nasturtium and carrot, and for several years I have planted garlic bulbs between my tomato plants to protect them from red spider mites. Though not containing fungicidal elements, tomatoes will protect roses against black spot.

The active principle of tomato leaves is *solanine*, a volatile alkaloid which at one time was used as an agricultural insecticide. To make a spray for roses: Make a solution of tomato leaves in your vegetable juicer, add 4 or 5 pints of water and a tablespoon of cornstarch. Strain and spray on roses where it is not convenient to plant tomatoes as companions. Keep any unused spray refrigerated.

The odor of butyl mercaptan, the defense spray of the skunk, is neutralized by tomato juice.

Unlike most other vegetables, tomatoes prefer to grow in the same place year after year. Stinging nettle growing nearby improves their keeping qualities, and redroot pigweed, in small quantities, is beneficial, too. Since they are heavy feeders give them ample quantities of compost or decomposed manure. Mulch and water in dry weather to maintain soil moisture and stave off wilt disease and blossom end rot. But never water tomatoes from the top. Water from below and water deeply. Tomatoes are inhibited by the presence of kohlrabi and fennel.

Root excretions of tomatoes have an inhibiting effect on young

basil, green + purple for flavor

6-8 weeks the outside fireballs early)

The skunk's protection, butyl mercaptan, can be neutralized with tomato juice. They have some benefit, however, in keeping large insects and mice in check.

apricot trees and don't plant tomatoes near corn, since the tomato fruitworm is identical with the corn earworm. Don't plant near potatoes, either, since tomatoes render them more susceptible to potato blight.

If you smoke, be sure to wash your hands thoroughly before you work in your garden, for tomatoes are susceptible to diseases transmitted through tobacco.

Triticale (*Triticale*). The International Wheat and Maize Center of Mexico has produced a new grain, triticale, by crossing wheat and rye, gaining the high yield of wheat and the disease and drought-resistance of rye. This was accomplished by the tedious process of cross-fertilization among different species. By nurturing the resulting embryo and chemically causing its chromosomes to duplicate themselves, they succeeded in producing fertile plants

Triticale is a man-made cross of wheat and rye and it will produce two or three times the yield of either of its parents. Though developed in Mexico it will grow anywhere that wheat will.

bearing the characteristics of both parents. A delicious bread made from triticale is now obtainable in many grocery stores throughout the Southwest. The flour's baking qualities are better than rye's.

Triticale (pronounced trit-i-kay-lee) as a man-made cross derives from the scientific names for wheat and rye, "triticum" and "secale." It has a higher protein content and protein efficiency ratio than either wheat or corn—comparable to soy concentrate—and it is also higher than wheat in lysine and methionine, two of the life-sustaining amino acids. Triticale has shown the ability to produce two or three times as much per acre as either wheat or rye and can be grown anywhere in the world where wheat is found. The grain is being improved constantly as new strains are developed at various experiment stations throughout the country.

Tulip (*Tulipa*).   Between 1634 and 1637 tulips became so fashionable in Holland that the craze was called "tulipomania," and the bulbs brought fantastic prices. The name comes from a Turkish word for "turban."

Though they are sun lovers, tulips grow better in the North than in the South, for the bulbs need a period of cold. Since mice like to eat the bulbs it sometimes is advisable to plant them in a small wire cage sunk in the earth and covered with soil. Scilla bulbs may also be planted with them as a protection against mice. Do not plant tulips near wheat, as they discourage its growth.

Turnip-Rutabaga (*Brassica rapa* and *Brassica napobrassica*). An accident discovered that hairy vetch and turnips are excellent companions. Turnip seeds became mixed with the vetch that a gardener planted and they came up as volunteer plants. He found the turnip greens were completely free of the aphids which usually infest them, apparently because the vetch provided shelter for ladybugs which feast on aphids. Elsewhere it has been found that wood ashes around the base of turnip plants will control scab.

I find peas planted near turnips are mutually benefitted. Turnip and radish seed mixed with clover will bolster the nitrogen content of the soil. In your crop rotation it is good to follow the heavy feeders with light feeders such as turnips and rutabagas.

Turnips dislike hedge mustard and knotweed, and do not rotate them with other members of the cabbage family such as broccoli or kohlrabi. A naturally-occurring chemical compound in turnips when synthesized is deadly to aphids, spider mites and houseflies, German cockroaches and bean beetles.

Rutabagas take much the same culture as turnips but require a longer growing season.

Two-level Planting. Vegetables which occupy different soil strata often make good companions. Among these are asparagus with parsley and tomatoes, beets with kohlrabi, beets with onion, leeks with vine plants, garlic with tomatoes, carrots with peas and strawberries with bush beans.

Many combinations like this are possible, enabling the gardener with little space to virtually double the yield of his garden, and at the same time improve the health and flavor of the vegetables planted together.

But do not plant together plants that are competing for the same space and light, such as sunflowers and pole beans, or plants whose root excretions react unfavorably on each other, such as carrots and dill.

Two Season Planting. Gardeners in areas which have a long growing season may find both a spring and fall garden possible. In the fall I can grow cauliflower, broccoli, Brussels sprouts, cabbage, collards, lettuce, radishes and English peas, and they are practically insect-free. Some of the vegetables which require a long growing season to head up are a complete failure for me if planted in the spring, because of the hot midsummer conditions. I cannot give you exact dates; this has to be worked out by area according to where you live, but is well worth trying experimentally.

In many places early-planted squash is more likely to withstand borers which lay their eggs in July. Where I live, we have a rule: "Plant squash and cucumbers the first day of May before the sun comes up and they will be free of beetles." I also find that fall-planted squash often escapes insects as well.

Radishes and cabbage may escape root maggots by careful timing. The Hessian fly's attacks on winter wheat may be avoided if the wheat is sown after the first week in October, when the fly is no longer active.

South Texas cotton farmers have found they can control the pink bollworm without insecticides by carefully establishing deadline dates for both the planting of cotton and destroying the stalks after harvest.

Observe when insect infestations are worst on certain crops, and plant either earlier or later than you have in the past.

V

Valerian (*Valeriana officinalis*).   This herb is good anywhere in the garden, particularly to give vegetables added vigor. It is rich in phosphorus and stimulates phosphorus activity where grown; it is attractive to earthworms and therefore particularly useful in the compost pile.

It is thought that the Pied Piper of Hamelin used valerian to clear the town of rats, yet many gardeners find it attracts cats, which love to nibble the leaves and roll against them. The Universal Herbal of 1820 states: "It is well known that cats are very fond of the roots of valerian; rats are also equally partial to it—hence rat-catchers employ them to draw the vermin together."

Valerian enjoyed great prominence in Colonial days as a drug plant, the strangely-scented root being brewed into a tea. Since the oil of valerian does have an effect on the central nervous system, the tea should not be drunk too often, yet many think it enhances and strengthens their psychic ability.

Cold tea is made by this rule: 1 level tsp. valerian put to soak in one cup cold water. Cover and place in cold place for 12 to 24 hours. Strain and drink about one hour before retiring.

Venus Flytrap (*Dionaea muscipula*).   This hungry little plant, which captures its own meals, must be grown in high humidity indoors or out. The insect traps on young plants, which develop in three to four weeks, consist of two leaves hinged in the center when open and when closed, forming a pouch in which the trapped insects are digested. When a leaf has caught several insects it withers and dies, but new ones take its place. Venus flytrap grows naturally in bogs where the soil lacks available nitrogen, and thus the insects take the place of nitrogen in the plant's diet.

Vertical Gardening.   If you have a fenced garden here is an opportunity for both beauty and increased productiveness. Many plants take kindly to climbing, cucumbers (such as Burpee *Burpless*) growing longer and straighter when trained on a fence. Scarlet runner beans climb rapidly and make a beautiful as well as tasty display. I plant these with my chayotes which bear good-tasting and attractive fruit in September.

Morning glories and pole beans do well together, and rambling roses are happy with gourds. When the roses are gone the gourds will bear attractive blossoms and fruits without damage to the roses. If you grow the birdhouse type of gourd these will be a bonus for your garden, dried and hung the following season to attract birds.

You might follow Oriental practice to relieve the somber dark green of pines by allowing clematis to grow into the trees, particularly the white ones which form huge panicles of scented flowers in late fall.

If you don't have a fence, try a tepee or wigwam made of four or more poles fastened together near the top and with soft wire or twine tied from pole to pole. The growing plants are trained to the poles by tying loosely. When they reach the top, pinch out the growing point of each plant, causing them to produce side shoots. This system is very good for vining squash. Soon the wigwam will be covered with a mass of attractive flowers, bright green leaves and squashes.

Vetch (*Vicia*).   Vetch, a relatively slow-growing perennial, is a good companion for oats and rye. Plant fast-growing rye or oats as a "nurse crop" to provide shade and check competitive growth. However, if this is done, the vetch should be planted more thinly than ordinarily or the annual nurse crop may be choked out by the sturdy perennial. Fall-planted vetch is one of our most valuable green manure crops. Being a legume it enriches the soil with both nitrogen and humus.

W

Wallflower (*Cheiranthus cheiri*).   A spray of rhubarb leaves will protect wallflowers against clubroot. Boil the leaves in water and sprinkle it where the wallflower seeds are to be sown. Wallflowers are believed to be beneficial to apple trees.

Walnut (*Juglans nigra*).   Black walnut trees are known to produce a substance called *juglone* which is washed from the leaves to the soil, inhibiting the growth of many plants within the area where the trees grow. Cultivated plants not compatible with black walnuts are apples, alfalfa, potatoes, tomatoes, blackberries, azaleas, rhododendrons and heather. The butternut (*J. cinerea*) also seems to have this quality, but plants near it are less severely affected. See also SYCAMORE.

But the black walnut is not all bad. In addition to the delicious nuts, the tree's leaves scattered around the house or put in the dog kennel will repel fleas.

A Russian remedy to prevent sunburn is to rub freshly-ground walnut leaves on the skin. The dark juice of walnut hulls applied to ringworm is said to heal the scalp.

Many believe that toxicity is contained in the roots of black walnuts as well as in the leaves, and that because of this many plants will not grow near the tree. But right at the drip line of a large black walnut I have a bed of rainbow-colored iris, interplanted with daylilies, grape hyacinth and daffodils, none of which appear to be in the least affected.

Walnut, English (*J. regia*)   do not have the detrimental leaf and root excretions credited to black walnuts, but their shade makes it difficult to grow some plants nearby. Many of the fruit mints such as apple, orange, pineapple or spearmint will do well, however, as will angelica and sweet anise and other herbs which like filtered sunlight.

Water Hyacinth (*Eichhornia crassipes*).   This tropical American plant has "escaped" and is now growing profusely in the southern states, sometimes choking ponds and streams with its growth of floating leaves. The roots hang down in the water and receive the spawn of fish. The lovely violet flowers are large and showy.

If you live in an area where water hyacinth has gone wild, you will benefit both yourself and the waterway by dredging it out and using it for compost.

Water Lily (*Nymphia odorata*).   The American water lily, related to the lotus, sends long, stout leaf and flower stalks from the mud bottom of clear, shallow water. The beautiful flowers usually rise above the water on long flower stalks and may be as large as a foot across. In cultivation water lilies grow well in a mixed planting of other water plants. In the wild state they, too, sometimes threaten to choke shallow pools of water and should be dredged out and composted.

Watermelon (*Citrullus vulgaris*).   Watermelons are good to interplant with potatoes, particularly if the potatoes are mulched with straw. The hybrid seedless watermelons, which set no pollen, will produce better if planted with a good pollinator such as *Sugar Baby*. Watermelons need plenty of sunshine, so do not plant them with or near other tall-growing vegetables.

Wax.   Evaporation would cause many plants to die if they did not have a waterproof surface. This common waterproofing on plant leaves is a wax which is produced within the leaf and is spread on its surface to form a protective wrapper, the reason some leaves are so shiny. The wax, however, does not cover the tiny pores, which are the means by which leaves interchange gases and water vapor with the air. Dust *will* cover these pores, the reason it is so important to keep the leaves of house plants clean.

This wax coating on leaves serves different purposes in different plants. It also may protect a plant chemically from some types of fungi but encourage the growing of others. It also may cause fungal spores to slip off a leaf before they gain a foothold—another reason for keeping house plants clean. The wax on some leaves contains odors and flavors which are characteristic of a particular kind of plant.

A study of the cabbage family by the Connecticut Agricultural Experiment Station shows that approximately 30 compounds make up the wax that causes the leaves to shine and allows them to shed water. Research is now taking apart the plant waxes to determine how they are made.

Weeds.   Someone once said, "A weed is a plant out of place," but I am inclined to go along with Ralph Waldo Emerson who believed, "a weed is a plant whose virtues have not yet been discovered." Weeds wisely used are some of our most important companion plants. Of course, they never should be allowed to overwhelm the food plants, but a few left here and there may surprise you by the influence they exert.

The extensive root growth of weeds penetrates the subsoil, breaking it up and making it easier for the roots of crop plants to go farther than usual as they search for water and nourishment. A few weeds are useful in shading the ground to keep seedling vegetables from drying out in the sun's heat. Meanwhile moisture from the subsoil will travel by capillary action up the outside of the weed roots to a level where the young vegetables can use it.

Deep divers such as pigweed, lamb's quarters and thistles bring up minerals from the lower soil by way of their stalks and leaves. When these weeds are turned under, the minerals become available to shallower-rooting crops. Minerals, along with trace minerals which may become exhausted under a succession of crops, and which might otherwise be leached away, thus are retained.

Another interesting fact is that weeds seem to accumulate the nutrients in which a particular soil is deficient. Such weeds as sheep sorrel and plantain, which thrive best in acid soil, are rich in alkalinizing minerals such as calcium and magnesium. Bracken, which grows best in phosphorus-poor soil, is high in phosphorus. Turning these weeds under will release these minerals into the topsoil, again making them available to food plants.

Weeds also benefit the soil by conditioning it. Their extensive root systems leave fibrous organic matter which decays, adding humus to both topsoil and subsoil. Not only this, but they also leave channels for drainage and aeration. The root systems of dandelions when decomposed provide subterranean channels for earthworms which, in turn, enrich the soil with their castings. Soil texture is vastly improved and soil-inhabiting bacteria will multiply enormously.

Learning to read weeds can be very useful, for they are excellent indicators of the type of soil they select to grow on.

Weeds that delight in acid soil, and also indicate increasing acidity, are the docks, fingerleaf weeds, lady's thumb and sorrels. Horsetail indicates slightly acid soil as do hawkweed and knapweed.

Weeds that indicate a crust formation and hardpan are the penny cress, morning glory, horse nettle, field mustard, camomiles, quack grass and pineapple weed.

Weeds most likely to occur on cultivated land are chickweed, buttercup, dandelion, lamb's quarters, plantain, nettle, prostrate knotweed, prickly lettuce, field speedwell, common horehound, celandine, mallows, rough pigweed and carpetweed.

Sandy soils are favored by arrow leaved wild lettuce, yellow toad flax, ononis, partrige pea, broom bush, flowered aster and most goldenrods.

On alkaline soils we are apt to find sagebrush and woody aster, while limestone soils grow field peppergrass, hare's ear mustard, wormseed, Canada blue grass, cornelian cherry, penny cress, Barnaby's thistle, mountain bluet, yellow camomile and field madder.

If a plot of land grows healthy weeds it will probably grow good vegetable crops, too. Let the weeds reach full growth but cut them before they go to seed. Let them wilt a few days and then plow them under for green manure.

You may even find it helpful to your compost pile to bring in extra weeds such as those cut by the highway department along public roadways. This largesse often includes such items as nettles, sunflowers, yarrow and sweet clover. These should be thoroughly composted to kill their seeds before being placed on the garden.

Weeds are not necessarily our enemies. With good management they may well become friends and co-workers.

Wheat (*Triticum vulgare*).   There are two stories about the origin of wheat, both extremely interesting. The first is that bread wheat appeared around 8000 B.C. when wild wheat by accidental cross-pollination apparently formed a hybrid with a type of "goat grass," resulting in much plumper grains. This new plant, called "emmer," again crossed with goat grass, forming an even more luxuriant hybrid. Because the husk of this grain was so tight that the whole grain would not scatter to the wind as other grass seeds do, the continued existence of "wheat" was dependent upon man, and thus bread wheat came into being.

The Theosophists believe that mankind at a certain stage in his development was assisted by some high initiates coming from the planet Venus. They believe that these advanced beings not only gave moral and social guidance to man but also brought with them wheat grains to supply a better cereal, bees to produce honey and fertilize flowers, and ants. Rye, they think, was produced by man in imitation of wheat by selective breeding. Oats and barley are thought to be hybrids brought about by crossing with earthly grasses.

In some regions poppies spring up and become a weed in wheat fields. They should not be allowed to spread, for they check the wheat's growth. On the other hand, camomile permitted to grow in very small ratio (1 to 100) with wheat is beneficial, while in larger amounts it's harmful. Wheat will be increased by the presence of maize.

The growth of wheat is adversely affected by cherry, dogwood, pine and tulip, as well as proximity to the roots of sorghum. Canada thistle and field bindweed are harmful to both wheat and linseed.

I have grown a good stand of winter wheat by sowing it in the fall on my Bermuda grass lawn. In our mild climate it grows intermittently all winter, heading about the last of June. After it is harvested, the Bermuda grass takes over again and you would never know the wheat had been there. I don't know if this would work with other lawn grasses or not.

If you do make a sowing of winter wheat, avoid the Hessian fly by sowing it late, timed according to when this fly appears in your area.

White Fly (*Trialeurodes vaporariorum*).   White fly is one of the insects known to thrive on certain shortages of minerals in the soil, and experiments have shown that greenhouse white flies attack tomatoes only when phosphorus or magnesium are deficient in the soil.

Botanical controls include nasturtium, particularly good to grow in greenhouses with tomatoes. Oak leaves burned in a greenhouse for a half hour period is helpful, and nicotine may be used as a spray.

White fly can be controlled biologically by a small parasite called *encorsia formosa*, (from Greenhouse Bio-Controls, 61 Horvath St., Kingsville, Ontario, Canada). Ladybugs also are a control, as are aphis lions.

White Hellebore (*Veratrum album*).   White hellebore is a member of the lily family whose roots and rhizomes contain insecticidal materials. It becomes less toxic upon exposure to light and air and has little residual effect, making it less poisonous to use than other materials.

The use of white hellebore is centuries old. The Greeks mixed it with milk to kill flies, and it was a favorite remedy of the Romans against mice and rats. Today it is used to control many leaf-eating insects such as sawflies which attack ripening fruit, and also for slugs and cabbage worm.

Wild Carrot (*Daucus carota*).   Wild carrot does not always indicate bad soil, for its deep taproot implies a deep soil capable of good cultivation. A rich crop indicates a soil worth improving for crops. But it can become a pest, so prevent it from seeding by cutting the plant close to the ground shortly after pollination. Do not cut too early or many plants will spread out from the root.

Wild Cherry (*Prunus Pennsylvanica*).   The wild bird, pin or red cherry grows from Newfoundland to Georgia and west to the Rocky Mountains in rocky woods, forming thickets which are valuable as nurse trees. It provides berries for birds and nectar-laden flowers for bees, so it can scarcely be called worthless, even though it is a short-lived tree. Wild cherry often springs up in burned-over districts where its bird-sown pits take root, the young trees sheltering new pines and hardwoods.

The wild black cherry (*P. serotina*) is sometimes called the rum cherry. A tonic is derived from its bark, roots and fruit, and brandies and cordials are made from its heavy-clustered fruit, which hang until late summer, turning black and losing their astringency when fully ripe. The wild black cherry makes an attractive shade and park tree, too.

The wild black cherry and the chokecherry (*P. virginiana*) are both of value to attract birds. Unfortunately the tent caterpillar favors them to lay its eggs, making the trees unpopular with farmers. The egg rings in the outer smaller branches are easily seen and removed.

Wild Morning Glory.   We have it from the Indians that wild morning glory was beneficial to corn, but if allowed to go to seed it can become a great pest, coming up for years afterward. It may be killed out by spraying a little white vinegar into the center of each vine.

Wild Parsnip (*Pastinaca sativa*).   Wild parsnip is a nourishing food plant which will give a good yield even on poor soils, but it soon becomes a weed and is hard to eradicate. The cow parsnip (*Heracleum lanatum*) is poisonous.

Wild Radish (*Paphanus raphanistrum*).   Wild radish spreads quickly in soils worn out from growing too many grain crops and depleted in nitrogen. It flourishes well, especially in wet years, where manure is scarce and potassium fertilizer abundant. Nevertheless cattle are very fond of it, and it produces a good honey as well as an oil from the seed.

Wild Rose (*Eglantine*).   When this pretty weed migrates from hedgerows to pastures it indicates the pasture has not been grazed adequately and needs mowing and harrowing. The prickly canes are troublesome to sheep and cattle but do not particularly bother goats, which love all kinds of rose bushes. To eradicate, cut the canes while they are still soft.

Wild Strawberry (*Fragaria*).   Wild strawberries are small, but have a delicious flavor quite unlike any others. Their presence in pasture land is an indicator of increasing acidity.

Willow (*Salix*).   The tough and fibrous roots of willow are useful in binding the banks of streams that may erode. Nature seems to have designed them specifically for this purpose, for wherever a twig lies upon the ground, it will strike root at every joint if the soil is sufficiently moist. The wind often breaks off twigs and the water carries them downstream where they lodge on banks and sand bars which soon become covered with billows of green.

For thousands of years the bark and leaves of the willow have

yielded resins and juices which eased the aches and pains of rheumatism and neuralgia or alleviated the distress of fevers. In the
1820's *salicin*, the active principle of willow bark, was isolated, and
in 1899 a synthetic derivative gave the world aspirin.

Windbreaks.   Before planting a windbreak study your land carefully and put it where it will do the most good. Consider prevailing wind directions and the location and relationship of your
buildings to the area you want protected. Most often they are
planted across the west and north sides of a property, but of course
there are exceptions to this rule depending on the configuration of
the land and the winds.

Do not plant your screen too close to the garden, for if the windbreak is to consist of trees and shrubs they will rob the soil of
moisture and nutrients. If you have sufficient land plant the windbreak at least 50 feet from field crops. Very possibly you do not
have this much room but be as generous as you can.

The protective factor of a windbreak is 20 times its height. Thus
a 10-foot screen would give you protection up to 200 feet down-
wind from it. You will also receive protection for several feet in
front of the tree belt because it causes the air to back up and act as
an invisible wall before it hits the planting of trees. Not the least
of its uses is to hold down soil against heavy winds and to keep
snow from drifting over walks and driveways. It may even help
you to reduce fuel bills.

In the prairie regions in particular, shelterbelt plantings have
a marked influence on local climate, especially if they are placed at
right angles to prevailing winds. A chain of such belts checking
movement of the air, causing a slowing down of wind velocity
even before the windbreak is reached, starts up a whole chain of
favorable climatic influences. These influences, such as a reduction of evaporation, by increasing the humidity of the air increase
the yield of crops grown under the protective influences. (See
HEDGES and VERTICAL GARDENING.)

Witch Hazel (*Hamamelis virginiana*).   The witch hazel is a stout,
many-stemmed shrub or small tree, characteristically an under-

growth of larger trees. American Indians were the first to use the bark of the witch hazel for curing inflammations. An infusion of the twigs and roots is made by boiling them for 24 hours in water to which alcohol then is added. The extract distilled from this mixture is used for bruises and sprains and to allay the pain of burns.

Perhaps the alcohol is the effective agent, for chemists have failed to discover any medicinal properties in either bark or leaf —yet who knows, they may still find it.

The tree has the peculiar property of throwing its seeds, particularly in dry, frosty weather. This does for the parent tree what the winged seeds of other, taller trees accomplish.

Witch hazel gets its names from the fact that superstitious English miners once used the forked twigs as divining rods.

Wood Ashes.   Wood ashes sprinkled around the base of cauliflower and onion plants are a popular remedy to control maggots, and to use against clubroot, red spider, bean beetles and scab on beets and turnips, as well as aphids on peas and lettuce. They are good, too, around such plants as corn, which need to develop strong stalks.

A thin paste made of wood ashes and water and painted on the trunks is used to control tree borers. A handful each of wood ashes and hydrated lime, diluted with two gallons of water, makes a spray for the upper and lower sides of cucurbit leaves to control cucumber beetles.

Just what *are* wood ashes? The food of trees comes from the air and the soil. Dry a stick of wood and the water leaves it; burn it and the ashes remain. The water and the ashes came from the soil. That part which came from the air passed off in gaseous form with the burning. The vast amount of carbon which the body of a tree contains came into its leaves as carbon dioxide. The soil furnished various minerals, which were brought up in the crude sap. And most of these valuable minerals remain as ashes when the wood is burned.

Woodchuck.   If woodchucks are a problem spray the plants they are nibbling with a solution of water and hot pepper.

Woodruff, Sweet (*Asperula odorata*).   Sweet woodruff is an excellent ground cover, particularly under crab apple trees. While it will grow in the sun, the foliage is darker green and much more abundant if it receives shade at least half of the day.

Wormwood (*Artemisia absinthium*).   Particularly the variety, *cineraria*, will keep animals out of the garden when used as a border. It's a good repellent for moths, flea beetles and cabbage worm butterfly. It discourages slugs if sprayed on the ground. Fleas on cats and dogs may be dislodged with a bath of wormwood tea.

Several artemisias are useful drugs for their vermifugal or insecticidal properties, the most important being *artemisia cina*, which yields the drug santonia or santonin from the flower heads, and is used for the expulsion of intestinal worms. It is also an ingredient of Absorbine Jr.! *A. absinthum* is used for the same purpose, and also provides an ingredient of the absinthe liqueur, which has been found damaging to the brain.

Wormwood inhibits growth of many plants, such as sage, fennel and caraway. But it also repels black flea beetles.

Many artemisias are of value as ornamentals, their cool, silvery beauty providing a fine contrast for flowers, such as red geraniums, of brilliant color. They do not attract honeybees, but small wasps seem to be frequent visitors. Keep wormwood out of the garden since most plants growing near it do not do well, particularly anise, caraway, fennel and sage. (See also ABSINTHIUM.)

Y

Yarrow (*Achillea millefolium*).   Yarrow is a plant of both mystery and history. For centuries the Chinese mystic has cast yarrow stalks when he consulted the I Ching.

According to the Bio-Dynamic book *Companion Plants*, yarrow has a definite effect on the quality of neighboring plants, not so much increasing their size as their resistance to adverse conditions

Yarrow's many benefits include repelling insect pests, while it increases the aromatic quality of other herbs. It also is said to help cuts to heal.

and thereby improving their health. It is a good companion for medicinal herbs, enhancing their essential oils and increasing their vitality.

Yarrow also gives nearby plants resistance to insects, perhaps because of its acrid, bitterly pungent odor.

Yarrow tea or yarrow hay are helpful to sheep, and I have given it to milk goats after kidding. It will grow almost anywhere and under any conditions and does not mind being walked upon. Where it grows in lawns and is cut by the mower, it simply spreads out in a low growth.

Yew (*Taxus*).   It is believed that yew trees grown near to rhododendrons are susceptible to root rot fungus, largely because of the acid soil needed for the rhododendrons. (See POISONOUS PLANTS chapter.)

Yucca (*Yucca*).   This plant has many names, the loveliest being the Spanish *candelaba de dios* or "candles of the Lord." The hardiest type, Adam's needle (*Y. filamentosa*) will grow in the North if given some winter protection.

Yuccas' great clusters of creamy, bell-shaped florets appear on the stiff, wood stalks ranging from three to 9 feet tall. In some species the immense symmetrical flower heads form the distinct shape of a cross. The blooms, which last from four to six weeks, are very fragrant, particularly so in the evening hours.

Yucca makes an excellent specimen plant as an accent for rock gardens, having the same cultural requirements as many others used for this purpose. It grows well with pine tree moss, an upright ground cover which grows six to 15 inches high with little tufts of needle-like foliage. Tall tulip varieties and daffodils interplanted around yucca in clumps add color while the moss is greening up.

In the Southwest many varieties of succulents and cactus grow well with yucca plants, which are valued for their ability to bind sandy soil, particularly in areas of high winds.

The Indians beat the roots of yucca in water, using the milky liquid produced for washing their hair. This shampoo is also thought to help the hair retain its natural color well into old age.

POLLINATION OF FRUITS AND NUTS

Pollination, as applied to fruit and nut trees, vines and bramble fruits, really is a matter of "companion planting," yet we seldom hear it called this.

For the gardener on a small lot, the site of his home orchard may be limited by necessity, the placement of trees being to a large extent dependent upon the overall landscape design. The homesteader, who has several acres, has at least a modest choice.

Few home gardens can accomodate more than two or three different kinds of fruit. To grow them successfully it is very important to consider varieties known to be self-fertile (also called "self-fruitful"), or which are good pollinators for the other types you wish to grow.

Since fruiting plants are more permanent than vegetables, their placement in the landscape design becomes most important. And often their usefulness may be doubled by considering also their ornamental and shade values.

Apples, plums, peaches and pears are such beautiful flowering trees that they may be used for the same design scheme as crab apples, dogwoods and redbuds. Pecans and walnuts (as well as apples and pears) make fine shade trees, too.

In areas where they grow well, blueberries will fit in nicely with other flowering shrubs such as forsythias, hydrangeas and spiraeas. A trellis or arbor becomes both useful and beautiful if bunch grapes or muscadines are planted to grow on it. Unsightly fences may be covered or a patio comfortably shaded if a few grape plants are placed thereon.

If your home site is not large enough for many trees, check around the neighborhood and list the fruit and nut trees you find there. Some of them may be good pollinators for trees you would like to plant.

Fruit and nut trees almost always do better if at least two of each variety are planted. For some varietes the need is imperative —they will bear scarcely at all without pollination help. But remember that pollination, important as it is, is only one factor in success.

While I won't go into the details of cultural practices here, it should be said that trees in a healthy growing condition will naturally derive more benefit from correct companion plantings. Healthy trees produce more pollen. And this applies to all trees, whether standard or dwarf types.

If you have room to set aside a definite orchard area, the first year you should do subsoiling, plowing, disking and grading well in advance of planting. If possible chooose a gently sloping site with good air and good soil drainage. There is nothing a tree dislikes more than a hardpan and wet feet.

Grow a nourishing cover crop such as rye, vetch, or soya beans and disk this in after well-rotted manure or compost has been spread. Allow time for its decomposition, for the trees do not like raw manure or organic matter around their roots. In a natural forest setting raw organic matter remains on top and only decomposed humus touches the roots.

Planting trees in early spring is the generally accepted practice but in the South or Southwest it is often possible to plant with good results in fall or early winter.

The actual planting of the trees comes after the soil has settled. Soil that absorbs water readily is the best, and you can test this by digging a 10-inch deep hole and filling it with water. If the hole drains completely within about eight hours, drainage may be considered satisfactory. However, if the water remains much longer, drainage is poor. To prevent root rot, work crushed rock, gravel or peat moss into the soil. Mixing compost with the soil will help in more ways than one.

For shrubs or bramble fruits the materials should be worked into the soil at least one foot deeper than planting depth. For trees, mix the additions to the soil about two or three feet deeper than the intended planting hole.

Shortly before planting, fill the hole with water and allow it to drain completely. This will prevent the surrounding soil from absorbing most of the water applied to the freshly-planted shrub or tree.

Maintaining a layer of mulch around new plantings also helps their growth, since it preserves moisture and in time becomes compost, providing plant nutrients.

Pollination is accomplished largely by bees, bumblebees and other beneficial insects so no sprays of any type should ever be used at blossoming time. In this limited space I cannot possibly list every variety of each fruit that will insure pollination, but there are a few general rules to follow for good results.

Apples.   All apples require a pollinator except *Golden Delicious, Jonathan, Red Rome Beauty,* and *Stark Tropical Beauty.* These four will bear well if grown alone, producing a good crop from self-pollination. *Baldwin, Gravenstein, Northern Spy, Rhode Island Greening, Arkansas Black,* or any of the winesap type including *Stayman* and *Staymared* should not be planted alone or be depended upon for pollination in a combination; they are either low or lacking in viable pollen. A red bud sport of any variety cannot pollenize that variety. Do not plant *McIntosh* and *Northern Spy* to pollinate each other.

Some good choices of varieties to plant together are *Lodi* (yellow-summer), *Yellow Delicious* (early fall), *Red Delicious* (mid-fall), *Red Stayman Winesap* and *Red Delight* (late fall).

Of all varieties, *Golden Delicious* (late) is probably the best pollinator, inasmuch as it blooms over a long period. Other apples which produce plenty of pollen and that may be relied on as "companions" in planting combinations are *Transparent, Idared* (early), *Grimes Golden, Delicious, Jonathan* and *Wealthy* (mid-season) and *Rome Beauty.*

If you have room only for one tree, there is still a way that you can have your favorite apple and pollinate it too. Graft a branch of a good pollinator somewhere on the host tree and this will serve your purpose. Apples like a near-neutral soil with a pH of 6 1/2 to 7.

Apricots. All apricots are self-fertile, but they too will benefit from cross-pollination to bear more heavily. Some of the best varieties include *Wilson Delicious, Stark Earli-Orange, Hungarian Rose, Early Golden, New Manchu* and *Moorpark. Royal,* a top variety, is now obtainable in dwarf trees.

Blackberries. Some self-unfruitful varieties of blackberries such as *Dallas* require cross-pollination. Others even though self-fruitful may benefit from the pollen-distributing visits of insects.

The flowers of blackberries are very attractive to their primary pollinators, honeybees. If a variety of blackberry is known to require cross-pollination, insure a sufficient supply of pollinators in large acreages by placing colonies of bees in or near the field.

Erect blackberries which do well under varying climate conditions include *Bailey, Darrow* and *Early Harvest.*

Do not grow blackberries near raspberries. Plant them in moderately acid soil, 5 to 5 3/4 pH.

Blueberries. Have at least two different varieties—any two—in a blueberry planting. Preferred varieties are *Tifblue, Briteblue, Delite, Woodard* and *Hombell* in southern regions. Further north try *Blueray, Coville* or *Jersey.* Blueberries like very acid (4 to 5 pH) and open porous soils, such as a sandpeat mixture with loam, with the water table 14 to 30 inches below the surface.

Boysenberries are sometimes called trailing or semi-trailing blackberries. Recommended varieties are *Lucretia, Thornfree* and *Thornless.*

Cherries.   All sour pie cherries are self-fruitful and have no pollination problems. *Early Richmond, Montmorency* and *Meteor* are all good varieties. A single tree may be planted and expected to produce well from its own pollen.

Sweet cherries all are *self-unfruitful* and will require another variety nearby to enable them to set fruit. There even are instances of pollen incompatibility among this group to further complicate things. However, if you include any one of *Van, Venus, Schmidt, Vista, Stark Gold* or *Black Tartarian* in combination you should have good results. *Napoleon, Lambert, Emperor Francis* and *Bing* will *not* pollinate each other. *Duke* cherries also are self-unfruitful.

Crab apple trees are often planted simply for their beauty. But they are self-fertile, and a good variety such as *Dolgo* will provide both beauty and fruit.

Figs.   Many people consider figs a tropical fruit, but there are varieties such as the *Dwarf Everbearing Fig for the North* (Burgess), which will do well elsewhere.

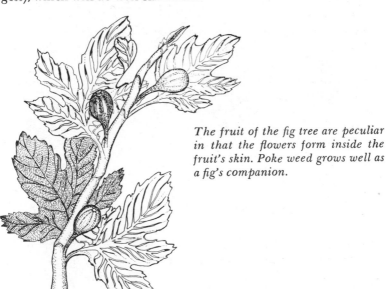

The fruit of the fig tree are peculiar in that the flowers form inside the fruit's skin. Poke weed grows well as a fig's companion.

Most figs offered by general nurseries are self-fertile. But some varieties will not mature their fruits unless the tiny female flowers are fertilized by pollen from a special kind of fig tree called a caprifig. Other varieties bear larger fruits if they are subjected to this process, which is known as "caprification." The pollen is transferred by a tiny wasp which spends part of its life in the fruits of the caprifig. In regions where Smyrna and other figs requiring caprification are grown, caprifigs are planted also.

One such variety requiring caprification is the *Calimyrna*, a type of Smyrna used to produce fruits for drying. Varieties that produce fruit either with or without caprification (the fruits are often larger if caprified), include *Adriatic, Beal, Brown Turkey, Magnolia, Texas Everbearing, Celeste* and *Mission*. Named varieties of caprifigs are *Stanford* and *Roeding Number 3*.

Grapes.   Bunch grapes such as *Concord, Fredonia* and *Niagara* are self-fertile, and one vine will give an abundance of grapes even if planted alone. Grapes like a moderately acid soil of 5 to 5 3/4 pH, and perhaps more than any other fruiting plant, particu-

Grapes are helped by an intercrop planting of legumes mixed with fifteen percent mustard (but cut this before it seeds). Hyssop nearby helps grapes, too.

larly important in moist, humid climates, need good air circulation to prevent fungus diseases such as mildew.

Grapes in their natural environment swing high in the trees, doing especially well if the tree happens to be an elm or a mulberry. Such grapes are seldom troubled by either brown rot or mildew. Since growing grapes in trees is impractical for most, the best solution perhaps is a terraced hillside unsuitable for other crops.

Try planting hyssop with your grapes for an increased yield, or use legumes as an intercrop. Cypress spurge is unfriendly, so do not let it grow nearby. To discourage the rose chafer keep grass out of the vineyard, its larvae feed on grass roots.

Muscadines (*Vitis rotundifolia*). Varieties include *Higgins* (large white) which requires a pollenizer, *Hunt,* which also requires a pollenizer but is the very best all-purpose black variety, and *Tarheel,* an excellent producer of pollen but which will bear alone. *Albemarle, Magnolia, Roanoke, Southland, Magoon* and *Cowart* are self-pollinating. Female plants needing pollination are *Nevermiss Scuppernong, Creek* and *Higgins Bronze.*

Muscadines as natives to southeastern United States do well under the high temperature and humidity found in this area, but they also are resistant to drought conditions and disease. Under favorable conditions they will live many years, but are not hardy in the northern United States because of low temperature conditions.

Mulberry. Mulberry trees have rather insipid-tasting fruits but can be very useful to lure birds away from cherries and berry plants. The birds seem actually to prefer mulberries.

The Russian mulberry is a rapid-growing tree that bears an abundant crop resembling blackberries, which may be made up into pies and jams.

Nectarines. Nectarines are self-fruitful. They also will pollinate peaches, and peaches nearby will help the nectarines to set a larger crop.

Peaches.   Most peaches are self-fruitful, but those requiring a pollinator are *Stark Hal-Berta Giant, Stark Honeydew Hale, J. H. Hale* and *Welcome.* Any other variety of peach will pollinate these, but the best pollinators are considered to be *Burbank July Elberta, Starking Delicious* and *Stark Early Elberta.* Peaches like a near neutral soil with a pH from 6 1/2 to 7.

Pears.   Almost all pears require other varieties nearby for a good fruit set, the exception under most conditions being *Duchess* and *Kieffer* which are self-fruitful. *Bartlett, Seckel, Grand Champion, Comice, Anjou, Starking Delicious, Magness, Buerre Bosc* and *Moonglow* all need cross-pollination.

Bartlett and *Seckel* are not compatible, and *Kieffer* is not always a good pollinator for *Bartlett.* A friend of mine had excellent success planting *Gellerts Butter* pear as a pollinator for his *Bartlett* trees. *Clapp's Favorite* is considered a good pollinator for most pear varieties.

If you live in an area where fire blight prevails it will pay you to plant resistant varieties. These are *Starking Delicious, Moonglow, Magness, Kieffer, Seckel, Tyson, Orient* and *Douglas.* Some suggestions for good companions: *Seckel* with *Tyson, Bartlett* with *Moonglow,* and *Magness* with *Duchess. Cope's Seedless* pear requires no pollenizer, but to retain its seedless qualities do not plant it near ordinary pear trees.

Persimmons.   There are two species of importance. The first, American persimmon (*Diospyros virginiana*) is native to a large part of the United States, and the second, the Oriental or Japanese persimmon (*Diospyros Kaki*), is a native of China and Korea. American and Japanese trees are not inter-fruitful.

The common persimmon is a small, low-growing tree perfectly adapted for the home-owner with limited space, since it is small, ordinarily attaining a height no greater than 40 or 50 feet. The inconspicuous greenish-yellow, urn-shaped male and female flowers are borne on separate trees.

*Persimmons come in dozens of culti-
vated varieties, which are considered
superior to the wild type native to
our Southeast.*

Japanese persimmons fall into three groups according to their
flower types:

Group I varieties produce only pistillate (female) flowers. These
varieties, called pistillate constants, *Eureka, Tani Nashi* and *Tam-
opan,* usually bear seedless fruit *without* pollination.

Group II varieties bear both staminate (male) and pistillate
flowers regularly and are called staminate constants.

Group III varieties bear pistillate flowers and occasionally
staminate flowers. This group is known as staminate sporadics.

Persimmons which are light-fleshed if seedless (dark if seedy)
are the *Gailey, Godbey, Hyakume, Okame, Yeman, Yeddo, Ichi,
Zingi, Taber 23* and *Taber 129. Gailey,* a profuse pollen producer,
is used for interplanting with varieties requiring cross-pollination.
A number of excellent grafted persimmon varieties are offered by
the Louis Gerardi Nursery. (SEE SUPPLIERS LIST.)

Plums.   All plums except *Giant Damson, Stanley, Green Gage*
and *Burbank Grand Prize* require pollination. These will fruit
alone. Some good plum combinations are *Redheart* with *Elephant
Heart, Ozark Premier* with *Santa Rosa, Burbank Grand Prize* with
Blufre, and *Ember* with *Giant Cherry. Redheart* generally is con-

sidered to be the most potent pollinator and is useful with any of the Japanese type (red) plums. Plums like a moderately acid soil of 5 to 5 3/4 pH.

Quince trees are self-fruitful.

Raspberries.   Raspberries, which like a near-neutral soil (6 1/2 to 7 pH), are self-fertile. Good varieties to plant are: Red: *Fallred, Latham, September, Southland, Sunrise, Taylor;* Black: *Allen, Blackhawk, Cumberland, Morrison;* Purple: *Amethyst, Clyde, Purple Autumn;* Yellow: *Amber* and *Fallgold.* Because of virus disease, black and purple raspberries should be planted no closer than 600 feet from red varieties. Do not plant any raspberries near potatoes since they make the potatoes more susceptible to blight.

Strawberries.   Almost all strawberries now sold, both June-bearing and ever-bearing, are self-fruitful. The "best" varieties vary from one area to another, and for more detail on varieties and culture reference see *The Complete Guide to Growing Berries and Grapes.* (See SUGGESTED READING.)

Strawberries will benefit if a few plants of borage, also a good attractant for honeybees, are grown near the bed.

In some sections growers plant strawberries as an intercrop in peach, apple, fig, orange or other tree-fruit orchards. When the orchard is first planted, strawberries may be set out and grown for several years before the trees need all the ground. The strawberries furnish some income from the land, or at least pay the expense of caring for the orchard. The intensive cultivation given strawberries is especially good for young orchards. Also because strawberries do not bear well unless moisture conditions are good, they will prove a good indicator of the orchard conditions.

NUT TREES

Almonds.   All varieties of the almond, which is not a true nut but belongs to the rose family, produce better if pollen from another tree is available. However, *Hall's Hardy* will produce reasonably well if grown alone. Peaches and almonds, being of the same family, will pollinate each other.

Black Walnuts.   Grafted varieties of these self-fruitful trees usually produce each year, while wild trees generally produce well only on alternate years, some only every third year. (See also WALNUT.)

Butternut has an inhibitory effect on plants within its immediate vicinity, but to a lesser degree than the black walnut. (See WALNUT.) Grafted butternuts are *Kenworthy* and *Mitchell.*

Cashew.   This native of Brazil has become naturalized in many tropical countries and will grow on sandy soils in Florida. Cross-pollination is not necessary.

Chinese Chestnut.   Plant two or more varieties for cross-pollination, some of the recommended varieties being *Orrin, Crain, Nanking* and *Abundance.*

English Walnuts.   Unless you live in a favorable climate you will probably be more successful with a tree of the carpathian type which will do well farther north. Grafted trees which bear well

are *Hansen, Helmle, Merkel, Colby, Lake, McKinster* and *Royal.*
Walnuts are monoecious—that is the male and female blossoms
are separate on the same tree. They are self-fertile but produce
better in plantings of several nearby.

Filberts and Hazels.   It is recommended that two, such as *Royal*
and *Barcelona,* be planted for cross-pollination and better crops.
Good grafted varieties of filberts and hazels also include *Potomac*
(Hyb.), *Reed* (Hyb.), *Bixby* (Hyb.), *Buchanan* (Hyb.), *Winkler
Hazel* (American), *Trizel* and *Betoka.* Two ornamental varieties
worthy of mention are *Bronze Leaf* (European) and *Corkscrew*
filbert.

Hickory.   The hickories, like the walnuts, have male and female
flowers growing separately on the same shoot of the current season's growth. Many varieties appear to be self-unfruitful, so it is
good practice to plant several varieties together to assure cross-
pollination. Grafted hickories for the North are *Harold, Ross, Ret-
zer, Wilcox, Scholl, Weschecke, Kaskaskia* and *Lindauer.*

Pecans in all varieties give no evidence of cross-incompatibility
and all will bear larger crops if two or more varieties are planted
together.
   Sometimes problems develop because the male and female flowers do not mature at the same time, but *Moore, Texas Prolific*
and *San Saba* have pollen available in time to pollinate the earliest flowers of any variety. *Moneymaker* and *Success* usually depend
on other varieties for pollination, while *Schley* and *Delmas* sometimes require pollen from other varieties. Good companions are
Stuart Papershell with *Schley Papershell, Major* with *Starking
Hardy Giant.*
   For more information on nut trees see my *Nuts for the Food
Gardener.*

FRUIT TREE CULTURE

Dr. Ehrenfried E. Pfeiffer, author of *The Biodynamic Treatment of Fruit Trees, Berries and Shrubs,* believed that a mixed culture in the orchard as well as in the garden helped to keep down insect pests. He advocated growing nasturtiums between fruit trees as a means of transmitting a "flavor" to the tree which made it disagreeable to insects. He considered it particularly effective when the flowers were grown under apple trees to repel woolly aphis. A washing down of the trees with nasturtium juice was recommended, if planting them was not possible.

Dr. Pfeiffer also suggested for orchard use stinging nettle, chives, garlic (against borers), tansy, horseradish and southernwood. Permanent covers considered beneficial are clovers, alfalfa and pasture grasses. Temporary crops to turn under for green manure are such biennial covers as mammoth clover, red clover and incarnate clover. He believed buckwheat useful on a light, sandy soil.

Though a mixture of red clover and mustards is considered ideal, Dr. Pfeiffer cautioned that mustard, while it sweetens the soil, can become a rapidly-spreading weed and for this reason should not be allowed to go to seed. Alfalfa hay, particularly if shredded or chopped, was thought to have special benefit as a mulch. He also recommended a paste for all fruit trees consisting of equal parts of cow manure, diatomaceous earth and clay to which horsetail tea is added, this mixture applied with a whitewash brush or with spraying equipment in the larger orchard.

A number of excellent preparations for fruit trees are obtainable from the Bio-Dynamic Farming and Gardening Association (address given at the back of this book). Bio-Dynamic 500, a humus preparation based on cow manure, is recommended for spraying on the ground. B.D. 501, the silica spray, is applied to the foliage of growing plants as a supplement to B.D. 500.

Here are some other helpful suggestions concerning fruiting plants:

Marigolds planted near apple trees or between rows of nursery stock will benefit the trees used in grafting and budding.

Wild mustard is beneficial to grapevines and fruit trees, but cut it before seeding.

Dandelions in the area of fruits and flowers will stimulate them to ripen quickly.

Chives improve the health of apple trees and will prevent apple scab. Use chive tea as a spray against apple scab and for powdery and downy mildew on gooseberries.

Ripening apples give off small amounts of ethylene gas which sometimes limits the height of nearby plants, but causes their flowers or fruit to mature earlier than normal.

Oats have an inhibitory effect on the growth of young apricot trees.

If you must replace a young fruit tree on the same spot where an old one has been removed, choose a different variety.

Garlic juice or the powdered extract contains a powerful anti-bacterial agent effective against diseases that damage stone fruits.

Do not place apples near carrots in a root cellar, as they may cause the carrots to take on a bitter flavor. If apples and potatoes are stored near each other, both will develop an "off" flavor.

POISONOUS PLANTS

Humans perhaps were given dominion over the birds and beasts and the lilies of the field (including thorn apple and castor bean) because they have (or should have) the ability to distinguish the good from the bad. We should know or should learn what may be safely eaten or touched, and that which is poisonous.

It would be virtually impossible to ban every plant that is inedible or drug-producing or even irritating to the skin. Moreover, many such plants are the source of valuable medicines or serve us well as natural insecticides when wisely and carefully used in our gardens.

Children should be taught which plants are harmful and which may be used or eaten or touched with safety. Caution the child old enough to understand about eating wild berries, fruits and nuts or chewing on bark, branches or stems. Watch younger children just as you keep them from running into the street or keep dangerous household preparations out of reach. For poisonous plants, whether present in your own garden or in fields nearby, *will* be encountered.

Since the beginning of time people the world over have lived close to hundreds of plants that can cause irritation, illness or even death. A few are seriously poisonous; a far greater number are moderately so, producing varying degrees of illness or irritation. Some cause dermatitis, hay fever or other illnesses as a result of the allergic sensitivity rather than the direct toxicity of the plant.

Dozens of these plants are such attractive garden flowers or

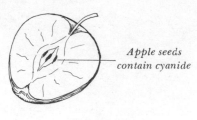
Apple seeds
contain cyanide

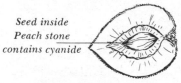
Seed inside
Peach stone
contains cyanide

Apples, peaches and castor beans
contain highly poisonous parts.

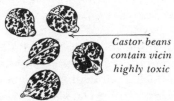
Castor beans
contain vicin
highly toxic

shrubs, greatly prized for their beauty or usefulness in landscaping, that many adults and most children do not realize their poisonous characteristics is a danger. Who would think, for instance, that "daffodils are dangerous." The beautifully-marked castor beans are a natural plaything for a small child, and little children often put things into their mouths. Yet for this poison there is no available antidote.

Even older children have been known to try the "nuts" inside a peach stone. How do I know? Because, as a child I tried one of these seeds which resemble almonds that I dearly loved. I didn't know that they contain cyanic acid and that a few of them could kill me. Fortunately the bitter flavor stopped me after the first bite. Parents can't think of everything to tell children not-to-do, so it is indeed fortunate that many dangerous plants do have an unpleasant taste.

But if my mother didn't know about the peach stones (and I kept my experiment a secret), there wasn't much else she didn't know about. She was a skilled herbalist, and I grew up with the salves and tonics she prepared and brewed from the plants she gathered.

She often told me of her adventures in the Indiana woods where she went to gather ginseng. Later, when she and my father were married, she transferred her herb-gathering activities to Kentucky, and still later, when the family came out to Oklahoma, then Indian Territory, she found literally new fields to conquer. She learned much herbal lore from the Indians who gave her the name "Hill-lea-tah-ha," meaning "one-who-thinks-good." In those days when there were few doctors and most people made their own medicines, her knowledge was greatly respected. And she was fortunate to be completely unaffected by poison ivy, an immunity which I too am happy to have.

To this day I still grow many of the plants my mother brought in from the woodland to use for their therapeutic or insecticidal properties. Until recently I did not think of them as "companion plants," though I was clearly aware of their effect when grown in proximity to flowers, fruits and vegetables.

While I have known since childhood most of the plants likely to be encountered in garden or woodland, there are many things about plants that I am still learning—for instance that some nonpoisonous plants have been contaminated by neighboring poisonous

Mistletoe usually won't be touched by animals, but it is poisonous. However, birds eat the berries without harm.

ones through a chemical chain. The poisonous plant absorbs selenium from the soil, something the "innocent" plants cannot do. In dying and decomposing, the poisonous plant leaves the selenium in a changed state, in a sense predigested, which causes the harmless plant during its next season's growth to draw the toxic substance into its own system.

I have no degree in botany, nor am I an expert on poisonous plants. Neither shall I try to cover *all* of them in this brief chapter. For those who are interested in pursuing the subject in greater detail note the two books listed under SUGGESTED READING. Here are only those plants which are most likely to be found in flower or vegetable gardens, or which may arrive, blown in by the wind or other means, as weeds. I have noted with a "D" those plants likely to cause dermatitis, a susceptibility that of course varies from person to person.

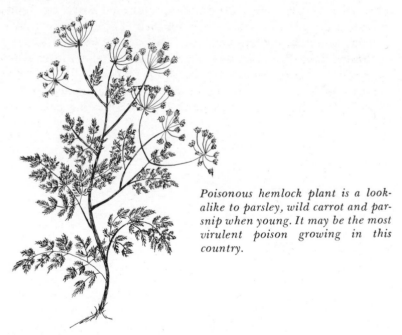

Poisonous hemlock plant is a look-alike to parsley, wild carrot and parsnip when young. It may be the most virulent poison growing in this country.

SCIENTIFIC NAME	COMMON NAME	POISONOUS PART OF PLANT
Abrus precatorius	rosary pea	A single rosary pea seed causes death.
Acokanthera spp.	bushman's poison	All parts very poisonous
Aconitum spp.	monkshood	All parts, especially roots and seeds very poisonous. Characterized by digestive upset and nervous excitement.
Adonis aestivalis	summer adonis	Leaves and stem
Aesculus spp.	horsechestnut, buckeye	Leaves and fruit
Ailanthus altissima	tree of heaven	Leaves, flowers; D
Amaryllis belladonna	belladonna lily	Bulbs
Anemone patens	pasque flower	Young plants and flowers
Arisaema triphyllum	jack-in-the pulpit	All parts, especially roots, (like dumb cane) contain small needle-like crystals of calcium oxalate that cause intense irritation and burning of the mouth and tongue.
Asclepias spp.	milkweeds	Leaves and stems
Asparagus officinalis	asparagus	Spears contain mercaptan, a substance which may cause kidney irritation if eaten in large amounts; young stems; D
Baileya multiradiata	desert marigold	Whole plant
Brunsvigia rosea	garden amaryllis, naked lady	Bulbs
Buxus sempervirens	common box	Leaves; D
Calonyction spp.	moonflower	Seeds
Cephalanthus occidentalis	buttonbush	Leaves
Cestrum spp.	cestrum, night-blooming jessamine	Leafy shoots
Cicuta	water hemlock	All parts fatal, cause violent and painful convulsions
Clematis vitalba	traveller's joy	Leaves
Colchicum autumnale	autumn crocus, meadow saffron	Leaves are very poisonous
Conium maculatus	poison hemlock	All parts

The handsome lily-of-the-valley has poisons in both leaves and flowers.

SCIENTIFIC NAME	COMMON NAME	POISONOUS PART OF PLANT
Convallaria majalis	lily-of-the-valley	Leaves and flowers very poisonous
Corynocarpus laevigata	karaka nut	Seeds
Crinum asiaticum	crinum lily	Bulbs
Crotalaria spp.	canary bird bush	Seeds
Cypripedium spp.	ladyslipper orchid	Hairy stems and leaves; D
Cytisus laburnum (see *Laburnum*)		
Daphne spp.	daphne	Bark, leaves and fruit fatal. A few berries can kill a child.
Datura spp.	angel's trumpet, thorn apple, jimsonweed	All parts cause abnormal thirst, distorted sight, delirum, incoherence and coma. Has proved fatal.
Delphinium spp.	larkspur, delphinium	Young plants and seeds cause digestive upset; may be fatal.
Dicentra spp.	Dutchman's breeches, bleeding-heart	Leaves and tubers may be poisonous in large amounts; fatal to cattle.
Dieffenbachia seguine	dumb cane	Stems and leaves cause intense burning and irritation of mouth and tongue. Death can occur if base of tongue swells enough to block the throat.

*The digitalis in foxglove is a power-
ful heart stimulant. It may be fatal if
the leaves are eaten.*

SCIENTIFIC NAME	COMMON NAME	POISONOUS PART OF PLANT
Digitalis purpurea	foxglove	Leaves cause digestive upset and mental confusion; may be fatal in large amounts.
Duranta repens	golden dewdrop	Fruits and leaves
Echium vulgare	blue weed	Leaves and stems; D
Euonymus europaea	European burning bush	Leaves and fruit
Eupatorium rugosum	white snakeroot	Leaves and stems
Euphorbia spp.	euphorbias, snow-on-the mountain, poinsettia	Milky sap; D. Leaves of poinsettia can kill a child.
Ficus spp.	figs	Milky sap; D
Fragaria spp.	strawberry	Fruit; D
Gelsemium sempervirens	yellow jessamine	Flowers and leaves; roots; D
Ginkgo biloba	ginkgo, maidenhair tree	Fruit juice; D
Gloriosa spp.	climbing lily	All parts
Hedera helix	English ivy	Leaves and berries
Helenium spp.	sneezeweed	Whole plant
Helleborus niger	Christmas rose	Rootstocks and leaves; D

SCIENTIFIC NAME	COMMON NAME	POISONOUS PART OF PLANT
Heracleum lanatum	cow parsnip	Leaves and root slightly poisonous; dangerous to cattle.
Heteromeles arbutifolia	toyon, Christmas berry	Leaves
Hyacinthus	hyacinth	Bulb causes nausea, vomiting; may be fatal.
Hydrangea macrophylla	hydrangea	Leaves
Hymenocallis americana	spider-lily	Bulbs
Hypericum perforatum	St. John's Wort	All parts when eaten; D
Ilex aquifolium	English holly	Berries
Impatiens spp.	impatiens	Young stems and leaves
Iris spp.	iris	Rhizomes; D. If eaten causes digestive upset but not usually serious.
Jasminum	jessamine	Berries fatal
Juglans spp.	walnut	Green hull juice; D
Kalmia latifolia	mountain laurel	Leaves
Laburnum vulgare	golden chain	Leaves and seeds cause severe poisoning; may be fatal.
Lantana spp.	lantana	Foliage and green berries may be fatal.
Laurus	laurels	All parts fatal
Ligustrum spp.	privet	Leaves and berries
Linum usitatissimum	flax	Whole plant, especially immature seed pods
Lobelia spp.	lobelia	Leaves, stems, and fruit; D
Lupinus spp.	lupines	Leaves, pods and especially seeds
Lycium halimifolium	matrimony vine	Leaves and young shoots
Macadamia ternifolia	queensland nut	Young leaves
Maclura pomifera	osage orange	Milky sap; D
Malus	apple	Seeds contain cyanic acid
Melia azedarach	chinaberry	Fruit, flowers and bark
Menispermum	moonseed	Berries (resemble small wild grapes) may be fatal if eaten
Myoporum laetum	ngaio	Leaves very poisonous
Narcissus spp.	narcissus, daffodil	Bulbs cause nausea, vomiting, may be fatal.
Nepeta hederacea	ground ivy	Leaves and stems
Nerium oleander	oleander	All parts extremely poisonous, affect the heart.
Nicotiana spp.	tobaccos	Foliage
Ornithogalum umbellatum	star-of-Bethlehem	All parts cause vomiting and nervous excitement
Oxalis cernua	Bermuda-buttercup	Leaves

SCIENTIFIC NAME	COMMON NAME	POISONOUS PART OF PLANT
Papaver somniferum	opium poppy	Unripe seed pod very poisonous
Pastinaca sativa	parsnip	Hairs on leaves and stems; D
Philodendron spp.	philodendron	Stems and leaves
Phoradendron spp.	common mistletoe	Berries fatal
Pittosporum spp.	pittosporum	Leaves, stem and fruit very poisonous
Podophyllum	May apple	Apple, foliage and roots contains at least 16 active toxic principles, primarily in the roots. Children often eat the apple with no ill effects but several may cause diarrhea.
Primula spp.	primrose	Leaves and stems; D
Prunus spp.	cherries, peaches, plums	Seeds and leaves; seeds contain cyanic acid.
Quercus	oaks	Foliage and acorns. Takes a large amount to poison
Ranunculus spp.	buttercup	Leaves; D. If eaten irritant juices may severely injure the digestive system.
Rhamnus spp.	coffee berry, buck-thorn	Sap and fruit; D
Rheum rhaponticum	rhubarb	Leaves; D. Large amounts of raw or cooked leaves (contain oxalic acid) can cause convulsions, coma, followed by death.
Rhododendron spp.	rhododendron, azalea	Leaves and all parts may be fatal

All parts of the lovely rhododendron are very toxic if eaten.

SCIENTIFIC NAME	COMMON NAME	POISONOUS PART OF PLANT
Rhus diversiloba	poison oak	Leaves
Ricinus communis	castor bean	Seeds fatal
Robina pseudo-acacia	black locust	Young shoots, bark and seeds.
Rumex acetosa	sour dock	Leaves
Sambucus canadensis	elderberry	Shoots, leaves and bark. Children have been poisoned by using the pithy stems for blowguns.
Saponaria vaccaria	cow cockle	Seeds
Sativus	autumn crocus	Vomiting and nervous excitement
Senecio mikanioides	German-ivy	Leaves and stems
Solanum dulcamara	European bittersweet	Leaves and berries
Solanum nudiflorum	black nightshade	Green berries poisonous but apparently harmless when fully ripe
Solanum nigrum	garden huckleberry nightshade	Unripe berries and leaves
Solanum pseudo-capsicum	Jerusalem-cherry	Fruit
Solanum tuberosum	Irish potato	Green skin on tubers
Tanacetum vulgare	common tansy	Leaves
Taxus baccata	yew	Foliage, bark and seeds fatal; foliage more toxic than berries
Thevetia peruviana	yellow oleander	All parts
Urtica spp.	nettles	Leaves; D
Veronica virginica	culvers root	Roots
Wisteria	wisteria	Mild to severe digestive upset. Children sometimes poisoned by this plant.
Zephyranthes spp.	zephyr-lily	Leaves and bulbs

FIRST AID IN EMERGENCIES

Poisonous Plants in the Garden, (see SUGGESTED READING), which includes much of the above information, suggests that in case of emergency the following first aid treatment be given:

Induce vomiting by giving a tablespoon of salt in a glass of warm water if the patient is conscious. *Do not attempt to give a drink if he is unconscious.* Keep patient warm and quiet and observe closely. Apply artificial respiration if patient is not breathing. Call physician immediately or take the patient to the closest hospital.

A Model Companion Garden, very much like the author's own (though smaller), has walkways around the fence inside for easy use of tiller. Note, too, how protective fence is used for such climbing plants as beans, cucumbers, peas and grapes.

Flowers add beauty to the garden but are chosen as well for their beneficial influences on crop vegetables and fruits. Note vegetable interplantings, too, in most of the rows. Perennials such as asparagus and horseradish are placed at the outsides to make tilling of the full garden easier.

SOURCES OF SUPPLY

Bio-Control Company, Route 2, Box 2397, Auburn, California 95603: *ladybugs.*

Bio-Dynamic Farming and Gardening Assoc., Inc., R.D.1, Stroudsburg, Pa. 18360: *sprays.*

Bountiful Ridge Nurseries, Inc., Princess Anne, Maryland 21853: *fruit trees, bramble fruits, nut trees, vegetable plants, seeds.*

Bower Industries, Inc., Perma-Guard Division, 1701 E. Elwood St., P.O. Box 21024, Phoenix, Arizona 85036: *diatomaceous earth.*

Casa Yerba, Box 176, Tustin, California 92680: *herbs.*

Burgess Seed and Plant Company, Galesburg, Michigan 49053: *general nursery plants.*

Eastern Biological Control Company, Route 5, Box 379, Jackson, New Jersey 08527: *praying mantises.*

Farmers Seed and Nursery Company, Fairbault, Minnesota 55021: *general nursery plants.*

Fairfax Biological Laboratory, Clinton Corners, New York, N.Y. 12514: *doom (Milky spore disease).*

Gothard, Inc., P. O. Box 332, Canutillo, Texas 79835: *Trick-O (trichogramma wasps), praying mantises.*

Greene Herb Gardens, Greene, R.I. 02827: *herbs.*

Gurney Seed & Nursery Company, Yankton, S.D. 57078: *general nursery plants.*

Henry Field, Shenandoah, Iowa 51601: *general nursery plants.*

Hydroponic Chemical Company, Copley, Ohio: *Japonex (Milky spore disease).*

Indiana Botanic Gardens, Box 5, Hammond, Indiana 46325: *white hellebore, other botanicals.*

International Minerals & Chemical Corp., Crop Aids Dept., 5401 Old Orchard Road, Skokie, Illinois 60076: *Thuricide (Bacillus thuringiensis)*.

Lakeland Nursery, Hanover, Pennsylvania 17331: *ladybugs*.

Louis Gerardi Nursery, R.R. No. 1, Box 146, O'Fallon, Illinois 62269: *fruit and nut trees*.

Mike Sankiw, Zoysia Farms, Dept. 431, 6414 Reisterstown Rd., Baltimore, Md. 21215: *zoysia grass*.

Monsanto Chemical Co., St. Louis, Mo.: *santocel, silica aerogel*.

Montgomery Ward, 618 W. Chicago Ave., Chicago, Ill. 60610: *ladybugs*.

Nichols Garden Nursery, 1190 North Pacific Highway, Albany, Oregon 97321: *rare herbs, vegetable seeds*.

Parks Flower Book, Geo. W. Park Seed Co., Inc., Greenwood, South Carolina 29647: *herb, vegetable seeds*.

Pine Hills Herb Farms, Box 144, Roswell, Georgia 30075: *herbs*.

Shumway, R. H., Seedsman, Rockford, Illinois 61101: *bulbs, herb, vegetable seeds, grasses, grains*.

Schnoor, L. E., Rough & Ready, California 95975: *ladybugs*.

Spring Hill Nurseries, Tipp City, Ohio 45366: *general nursery plants, sub-zero opuntia cactus, yucca, aloe vera, succulents, alliums*.

Stark Bro's Nurseries, Louisiana, Missouri 63353: *fruit and nut trees*.

Stokes Seeds, Inc., Box 548, Buffalo, New York 14240: *untreated seeds*.

Sterns Nurseries, Geneva, New York 14456: *general nursery plants*.

The Tanglefoot Company, 314 Straight Ave., S.W., Grand Rapids, Michigan 49500: *tree tanglefoot*.

Thompson-Hayward Chemical Co., P.O. Box 2383, Kansas City, Kansas 66110: *Biotrol (Bacillus thuringiensis)*

Twilley Seed Company, Salisbury, Maryland 21801: *seeds*.

Van Ness Water Gardens, 2460 North Euclid Ave., (Crescent West), Upland, Calif. 91786: *horsetail (equisetum), eel grass (vallisneria), water lilies*.

Vitova Insectary, Inc., P.O. Box 475, Rialto, California 92376: *lacewings (aphid lions), trichogramma wasps*.

William Tricker, Inc., 174 Allendale Ave., Saddle River, New Jersey 07458: *water lilies, eel grass, wild rice (zizania aquatica)*.

Wolfe Nursery, Highway 377 West, Stephenville, Texas 76401: *fruit and nut trees*.

SUGGESTED READING

Books and Articles

Biles, Roy E.; *The Complete Book of Garden Magic*, 1961, J. G. Ferguson Publishing Company, 6 N. Michigan Ave., Chicago, Illinois 60602.

Blanchan, Neltje; *Wild Flowers and Birds*, 1926, Doubleday & Company, Inc., Garden City, New York 11530.

Campbell, Stu; *The Mulch Book*, 1974, Garden Way Publishing, Charlotte, Vermont 05445.

Clarkson, Rosetta E.: *Herbs: Their Culture and Uses*, 1970, The Macmillan Co., 866 Third Ave., New York 10022.

Coon, Nelson; *Using Plants for Healing*, 1963, Hearthside Press, Inc., 381 Park Ave. South, New York, N.Y. 10016.

Creekmore, Hubert; *Daffodils Are Dangerous*, 1966, Walker & Co., 720 Fifth Ave., New York, N.Y. 10019.

Encyclopedia of Organic Gardening, 1974, Rodale Books, Inc., 33 E. Minor St., Emmaus, Pa. 18049.

Foster, Gertrude B.; *Herbs for Every Garden*, 1966, E. P. Dutton & Co., 201 Park Ave. South, New York, N.Y. 10013.

Gibbons, Euell; *Stalking the Good Life*, 1966; *Stalking the Healthful Herbs*, 1967; *Stalking the Wild Asparagus*, 1962, David McKay Company, Inc., 750 Third Ave., New York, N.Y. 10017.

Grimm, William Carey; *Home Guide to Trees, Shrubs and Wildflowers*, 1970, Stackpole Books, Cameron and Kelker Streets, Harrisburg, Penn. 17105.

Hunter, Beatrice Trum; *Gardening Without Poisons*, 1964, Houghton Mifflin Co., 1 Beacon St., Boston, Mass. 02108.

Jacob, Dorothy; *A Witch's Guide to Gardening*, 1965, Taplinger Publishing Co., 200 Park Ave., New York, N.Y. 10003.

214

Jaynes, Richard A., Editor, *Handbook of North American Nut Trees*, 1973, published by The Northern Nut Growers Assn., 4518 Holston Hills Road, Knoxville, Tenn. 37914.

Kingsbury, John M.; *Poisonous Plants of United States and Canada*, 1964, Prentice-Hall, Inc., Englewood Cliffs, N.J. 07632.

Koeph, H. H.; "The Living Soil Protects Plants," published in NATURAL FOOD AND FARMING MAGAZINE, 1963, Atlanta, Texas.

Koeph, H. H.; "Bio-Dynamic Sprays," from BIO-DYNAMICS No. 97, Winter, 1971, Bio-Dynamic Farming & Gardening Assn., R.D. 1, Stroudsburg, Pa. 18360.

Lehner, Ernst and Johanna; *Food and Medicinal Plants*, 1962, Tudor Publishing Co., 221 Park Ave. South, New York, N.Y. 10003.

Leyel, Mrs. C. F.; *Elixirs of Life*, 1970, Samuel Weiser, Inc., 734 Broadway, New York, N.Y. 10003.

Loewenfeld, Claire; *Herb Gardening*, 1965, Charles T. Branford Company, 28 Union St., Newton Center, Mass. 02159.

McCormick, Jack; *The Life of the Forest*, 1966, McGraw-Hill Book Co., 1221 Ave. of Americas, New York, N.Y. 10020.

McCurdy, Robert M.; *Garden Flowers*, 1926, Doubleday & Co., Inc., Garden City, N.Y. 11530.

ORGANIC GARDENING AND FARMING MAGAZINE (1968-1974, Incl.), 33 Minor St., Emmaus, Pa. 18049

Painter, Reginald H.; *Insect Resistance in Crop Plants*, 1968, The University Press of Kansas, 366 Watson Library, Lawrence, Kansas 66044.

Pharmacopoeia of the United States, Seventh Decennial Revision, published 1890 by the Committee of Revision, Philadelphia, Pa.

Philbrick, Helen and Richard Gregg; *Companion Plants and How to Use Them*, 1974, Devin-Adair Co., One Park Ave., Old Greenwich, Conn. 06870.

Pfeiffer, E. E.; *Weeds and What They Tell*, 1974, Bio-Dynamic Farming & Gardening Assn., Inc., 308 East Adams St., Springfield, Ill. 62701.

Pfeiffer, E. E.; *The Pfeiffer Garden Book*, 1974, Bio-Dynamic Farming & Gardening Assn., Inc., 308 East Adams St., Springfield, Ill. 62701.

Pfeiffer, E. E.; *The Art and Science of Composting*, 1959, R.D. 1, Stroudsburg, Pa. 18360.

Pfeiffer, E. E.; *The Biodynamic Treatment of Fruit Trees, Berries and Shrubs*, 1957, Bio-Dynamic Farming & Gardening Assn., 308 East Adams St., Springfield, Ill. 62701.

Riotte, Louise; *The Complete Guide to Growing Berries and Grapes*, Garden Way Publishing Co., 1974, Charlotte, Vermont 05445.

Riotte, Louise; *Nuts for the Food Gardener*, 1975, Garden Way Publishing Co., Charlotte, Vermont, 05445.

Rogers, Julia Ellen; *Trees*, 1926, Doubleday & Co., Garden City, New York 11530.

Tiedjens, Victor A.; *The Vegetable Encyclopedia and Gardener's Guide,* 1968, Bell Publishing Co., 419 Park Ave. South, New York, N.Y. 10016.

The Marshall Cavendish Illustrated Encyclopedia of Gardening, Editor Peter Hunt, 1970, Marshall Cavendish Corp., 111 W. 57th St., New York, N.Y. 10019.

World Book Encyclopedia, 1963, Field Enterprises Educational Corp., 510 Merchandise Mart. Pl., Chicago, Ill. 60654.

State Sources, Bulletins, Booklets, Pamphlets

CALIFORNIA: Bulletins from Agricultural Extension Service, University of California, 566 Lugo Ave., San Bernardino, Calif. 92410.

Poisonous Plants for the Garden, AXT-22, 1966.

Growing Herbs for Seasoning and Food, AXT-112, 1964.

CONNECTICUT: Connecticut Agricultural Experiment Station, New Haven, Conn. 06510.

Marigolds—A Biological Control of Meadow Nematodes in Gardens, by P. M. Miller and J. F. Ahrens, Bulletin No. 701, 1969.

NEW MEXICO: New Mexico State University, Box 2AE, Las Cruces, New Mexico 88003.

Triticale Production in New Mexico, Agricultural Experiment Station, Bulletin 625.

NEW YORK: Cornell University, Ithaca, New York 14850.

Allelochemics: Chemical Interactions Between Species, by R. H. Whittaker and P. P. Feeny, Reprinted from Feb. 26, 1971, Volume 171, The American Association for the Advancement of Science.

OKLAHOMA, University of Oklahoma, Norman, Oklahoma 73069.

Allelopathic Effects of Platanus Occidentalis, by Falah Abdul-Ghani Al-Naib and Elroy L. Rice, 1971.

Possible Role of Ambrosia psilostachva on Pattern and Succession in Old-Fields, by Robert L. Neill and Elroy L. Rice, 1971.

INDEX

A spray of sage, tarragon, thyme, or tansy accross plants will keep away the cabbage moths.

against pests - feverfew, tansy, marigolds, & nasturtiums

Grinding wastes
dolomitic limestone
Rock phosphate - Phospher
Green sand - potassium 20 -100 sq.